WITHDRAWN

Also by Peter Handke

The Ride Across
Lake Constance

AND OTHER PLAYS

DALE H. GRAMLEY LIBRARY
SALEM COLLEGE
WINSTON-SALEM, N. C.

PETER HANDKE

The Ride Across Lake Constance

AND OTHER PLAYS

Translated by MICHAEL ROLOFF
in collaboration with Karl Weber

FARRAR, STRAUS AND GIROUX / NEW YORK

PT
2668
A 5
A 274

This edition copyright © 1976 by Farrar, Straus and Giroux, Inc.

Copyright © 1966, 1967, 1969, 1970, 1973 by Suhrkamp Verlag

English translation of *Calling for Help* and *My Foot My Tutor* copyright © 1970 by Michael Roloff; of *The Ride Across Lake Constance* copyright © 1972 by Michael Roloff; of *Quodlibet* copyright © 1973 by Michael Roloff; of *They Are Dying Out* copyright © 1974 by Michael Roloff and Karl Weber; of *Prophecy* copyright © 1976 by Michael Roloff

All rights reserved

Amateur or professional performances, public readings, and radio or television broadcasts of these plays are forbidden without permission in writing. All inquiries concerning United States performing rights for *Prophecy*, *Calling for Help*, and *My Foot My Tutor* should be addressed to Kurt Bernheim, 575 Madison Avenue, Suite 502, New York, N.Y.; all inquiries concerning United States performing rights for *Quodlibet*, *The Ride Across Lake Constance*, and *They Are Dying Out* should be addressed to Toby Cole, 234 West 44th Street, New York, N.Y.

FIRST PRINTING, 1976

Printed in the United States of America
Published simultaneously in Canada by McGraw-Hill Ryerson Ltd., Toronto

DESIGNED BY HERB JOHNSON

Library of Congress Cataloging in Publication Data
  Handke, Peter.
    The ride across Lake Constance and other plays.
    CONTENTS: Prophecy.—Calling for Help.—My foot
  my tutor. [etc.]
    I. Title.
  PT2668.A5A274   832'.9'14   76–27655

Contents

Prophecy

Where to begin?
Everything is out of joint and totters.
The air quivers with comparisons.
No word is better than the other,
the earth booms with metaphors . . .
—OSIP MANDELSTAM

Four speakers (A, B, C, D)

A
The flies will die like flies.

B
The ruttish dogs will snuffle like ruttish dogs.

C
The pig on the spit will scream like a pig on the spit.

D
The bull will roar like a bull.

A
The statue will stand like a statue.

B
The chickens will scurry like chickens.

C
The madman will run like a madman.

D
The lunatic will howl like a lunatic.

A
The mangy dog will roam like a mangy dog.

B
The vulture will circle like a vulture.

C
The aspen leaves will quiver like aspen leaves.

D
The grass will quiver like grass.

AB
The house of cards will tumble like a house of cards.

AC
The bombs will strike like bombs.

AD
The ripe fruit will fall from the trees like ripe fruit.

BC

The water on the hot stone will hiss like water on a hot
stone.

BD

Those who are doomed to die will stand like those who are
doomed to die.

ABCD

The stuck pig will bleed like a stuck pig.

A

The average person will behave like an average person.

B

The bastard will behave like a bastard.

C

The man of honor will behave like a man of honor.

D

The opera hero will behave like an opera hero.

A

The stepchild will be treated like a stepchild.
The miracle worker will be awaited like a miracle worker.
The freak will be stared at like a freak.
The Messiah will be longed for like the Messiah.
The milch cow will be exploited like a milch cow.
The lepers will be shunned like lepers.
Hell will be hated like hell.
The shroud will be spread out like a shroud.
The mad dog will be shot like a mad dog.

B

The fool will prattle like a fool.
The parrot will prattle like a parrot.

The roaches will scurry from the light like roaches.
The snow in May will vanish like the snow in May.
The child will be happy like a child.
The miracle will happen like a miracle.
The corpse in the pool will swell up like a corpse in a pool.
The thunderclap will be like a thunderclap.

CD

The trooper will swear like a trooper.
The frog will leap like a frog.
Lightning will flash like lightning.
The thief will sneak off like a thief.
The horse will eat like a horse.
The school child will hide like a school child.
The splash in the water will be like a splash in the water.
The slap in the face will be like a slap in the face.
The viper will strike like a viper.

BCD

The wounded horses will rear up like wounded horses.
The jockey will be alert like a jockey.
The huskies will howl like huskies.
The Jew will haggle like a Jew.
The fish will wriggle on the hook like a fish on a hook.
The open wound will fester like an open wound.
The virgin will put on airs like a virgin.
The choirboy will walk like a choirboy.
The sailor will walk like a sailor.
The Spaniard will walk like a Spaniard.
Gary Cooper will walk like Gary Cooper.
Donald Duck will walk like Donald Duck.

A

The wet poodle will stand there like a wet poodle.
The poor sinner will stand there like a poor sinner.

The cow will stand before the new barn door like a cow before a new barn door.
The rooster on the dungheap will stand like a rooster on a
dungheap.

AB

The felled tree will crash like a felled tree.
The maniac will fight like a maniac.
The cat will slink around the hot soup like a cat around
hot soup.
The dogs will hide from the thunderstorm like dogs hiding
from a thunderstorm.
The roaring lion will stalk about like a roaring lion.
The wildfire will spread like wildfire.

ABC

The hyenas will howl like hyenas.
The nightwatchman will yawn like a nightwatchman.
The conspirators will whisper like conspirators.
The reeds in the wind will rustle like reeds in the wind.
The ostrich will bury its head in the sand like an ostrich.
The grass widow will tremble like a grass widow.
The rat will sleep like a rat.
The dog will die like a dog.

ABCD

The shoe will fit like a shoe on a foot.

A

The plague will spread like the plague.

B

The rose will smell like a rose.

C

The swarm of bees will buzz like a swarm of bees.

D

Your shadow will follow you like a shadow.

A

The tomb will be silent like a tomb.
The monument will stand like a monument.

B

A man will rise up like a man.
The cliff will stand in the surf like a cliff in the surf.

C

The cloudburst will approach like a cloudburst.
The ants will bite like ants.

D

The tidal wave will swell like a tidal wave.
The flock of frightened sheep will scatter like a flock of
                                                    frightened sheep.

A

The sand will run through your fingers like sand.

B

In the theater you will feel like a theatergoer.

C

One egg will resemble another as one egg another.

ABC

A scream will issue from the mouth of the crowd as out of
                                                    one mouth.

D
The organ pipes will stand like organ pipes.
The trumpets of the Last Judgment will ring out like the
trumpets of the Last Judgment.
The revelation will be like a revelation.

C
The mole will tunnel through the lawn like a mole.

B
The voice from another world will sound like a voice from
another world.

A
The avalanche will hurtle like an avalanche.
Those who have lost their senses will behave like people who
have lost their senses.

AB
The prophet will make faces like a prophet.
The angels will speak as with angels' tongues.
The moth will flutter to the light like a moth to the light.
The barn door will be open like a barn door.

ABC
The scales will fall from your eyes like scales falling from
your eyes.
The foreign body will be spewed out like a foreign body.
The rats will leave the sinking ship like rats leaving a sinking
ship.
God will step before mankind like God.

AB
The bear will sleep like a bear.

A

The wall will stand like a wall.

D

The cornfield will rustle like a cornfield.

DC

After the rain the mushrooms will mushroom like mushrooms
after the rain.

DCB

The nutshell will rock on the water like a nutshell on the
water.

DCBA

The migratory birds will flock like migratory birds.
Those who walk on a cloud will walk as if on a cloud.
Those who are struck by thunder will be like thunderstruck
people.
Those who are in seventh heaven will feel as if they were in
seventh heaven.
Those stung by a scorpion will leap up like those who are
stung by a scorpion.

AD

Ebb and flood will alternate like ebb and flood.
The fish in the water will flit about like fish in the water.
Water and fire will be compatible like water and fire.
Day and night will be as different as day and night.

B

You will live in clover like someone living in clover.

C

The dream will seem to you like a dream.

B
Eternity will seem to you like an eternity.

ABCD
But the fish in the sea shall be plentiful like fish in the sea.
But the sand at the shore shall be plentiful like sand at the
shore.
But the stars in the heavens shall be plentiful like stars in the
heavens.
But the people on earth shall be plentiful like people on
earth.

A
And the rabbits will multiply like rabbits.

B
And the germs will multiply like germs.

C
And the poor will multiply like the poor.

D
And a man like you and me will be a man like you and me.

A
Daily bread will be needed like daily bread.

B
Blood will be red like blood.

C
The wind will be swift like wind.

D
Poison will be yellow like poison.

DALE H. GRAMLEY LIBRARY
SALEM COLLEGE
WINSTON-SALEM, N. C.

A

Molasses will be sticky like molasses.

B

The fool will be gentle like a fool.

C

Life will be complex like life.

D

The sieve will be holey like a sieve.

A

The ultimate things will be unutterable like ultimate things.

B

The razor's edge will be sharp like a razor's edge.

C

The universe will be infinite like a universe.

D

The picky eater will be skinny like a picky eater.

A

The barrel will be round like a barrel.

B

The nigger will be uppity like a nigger.

C

The father will be to the son as father to son.

D

The ride in the jalopy will be bumpy like a ride in a jalopy.

A

The Pope will be infallible like the Pope.

B

The novel will be fantastic like a novel.

C

The movie will be unreal like a movie.

D

The needle in the haystack will be hard to find like a needle
in a haystack.

A

The night will be silent like the night.

B

Sin will be black like sin.

C

The soul will be inexhaustible like the soul.

D

The well will be deep like a well.

A

The sponge will be wet like a sponge.

B

The poet will be dreamy like a poet.

C

The others will be entirely like the others.

D
Death will be inevitable like death.

A
The morrow will be inevitable like the morrow.

B
The amen in the prayer will be inevitable like the amen in the prayer.

C
Something will be as inevitable as only something can be inevitable.

D
The peacock will be proud like a peacock.

ABCD
And the transformed will feel like those transformed.
And those who are turned into pillars of salt will stand there like ones turned into pillars of salt.
And those who are struck by lightning will fall like ones struck by lightning.
And the spellbound will listen like spellbound people.
And the paralyzed will stand like paralyzed people.
And the beckoned will come like beckoned people.
And the lame will stand like lame people.
And those struck by thunder will stand there like thunderstruck people.
And the sleeping will walk like sleepwalkers.
And those who have been called but not chosen will stand there like ones called but not chosen.
And the substitutes will feel like substitutes.
And the people by the mirror will look at themselves like people in front of the mirror.
And the newborn will feel like the newborn.

And the beaten will feel like beaten people.
And those who have been swallowed up by the earth will be
                like ones swallowed up by the earth.

A
The reality will become reality.

B
The truth will become truth.

AB
The ice will freeze like ice.

ABC
The ends will stand on end.

ABCD
The bottom will plunge to the bottom.

ABC
Nothingness will become nothing.

AB
The ashes will turn to ashes.

B
The air will turn to air.

A
The dust will turn to dust.

D
The weasel will be weasel-faced.

    C
    The feather will be feather-light.

B
Acid will be acid-fast.

A
Chalk will be chalk-white.

D
Butter will be butter-soft.

C
Lightning will be lightning-fast.

B
The hair will be a hairsbreadth thin.

A
Death will be deadly dull.

D
The dead will be deathly pale.

C
The dying will feel deathly ill.

B
Pitch will be pitch-black.

A
The heart will be heartsick.

D
The skin will be skin-deep.

C
The bloodsucker will be bloodthirsty.

B
The threads will be threadbare.

A
The stone will be stone-hard.

ABCD
Every day will be like every other.

Translated by Michael Roloff

Calling for Help

although the number of people who may participate in this *Sprechstück* is unlimited, it requires a minimum of two speakers (male or female). the speakers' objective is to show the way to the sought-after word HELP, a way that leads across many sentences and words. the speakers are playing the need for help without, however, being in a situation that really requires help; they are playing the need *acoustically*. while the way to the word help is being demonstrated, the sentences and words are not uttered with their usual meaning, but only to signify that help is being sought. while the speakers are seeking the *word* help they are in need of *help*; once having found the *word* help they no longer need any help. before they find the word they ask *for* help, whereas once they have found the word help they only speak *help* without needing to ask *for* help any longer. once able to shout help, they no longer need to shout *for* help; they are relieved that they can shout help. the word HELP has lost its meaning.

on their way to the word help, the speakers repeatedly approach the proximate meaning or only the acoustic proximity of the sought-after word: the respective NO-response that greets each attempt also changes according to the degree of proximity; the formal tension of the speaking increases; the course that this tension prescribes resembles, say, the rising and falling decibel curve during a soccer match; the closer one team gets to the goal of the other, the more the spectator noise increases, dying off again after each unsuccessful or impeded attempt to score, then swelling again, etc., until the word HELP is found during the final onslaught; then pure joy reigns among the speakers.

the spectators and listeners quickly recognize the speakers' objective. however, should the spectators indicate to the speakers, as spectators are wont to during punch-and-judy shows, that they know what the speakers need, and should they shout HELP, in that event the speakers, like performers who are threatened by the crocodile in a punch-and-judy show, won't understand what the spectators have in mind, but will understand the helpful shouts of HELP only as *genuine* distress calls, which only bother the speakers during their *play*. once the speakers have found the word help, it is repeated as a triumphant shout, so often that its meaning becomes an ovation to the *word* help. when the ovation becomes nearly unbearable, the mass chorus breaks off and a single speaker instantly speaks the word HELP by himself, neither expressing gladness with it nor that he is seeking help. the word HELP is uttered that way once.

the speakers also may drink COCA-COLA at intervals.

and in conclusion, while we think of all of you once more, we call on you and invite you to search with us for ways to mutual understanding, to deepened knowledge, to an open heart, to a fraternal life in the one truly world-embracing community of men: NO.

immediately after the assassination the authorities employed all available means to obtain a clear picture of the murder: NO. don't worry too much but enjoy the good times: NO. the claim that these persons were compelled to enter the plane is made up of thin air: NO. the dangers of missing the boat in one's profession are minimal at present: NO. those who come after you also want to use the towel: NO. the cripple can't be blamed for being a cripple: NO.

someone has escaped from death row: NO. the head of state has placed a wreath in the name of all the people: NO. unemployment has continued to recede: NO. a few cracks have become visible in the ice: NO. the teacher has reprimanded the unruly student: NO. the high pressure system has moved farther east: NO. an old proverb has something to say: NO. the wounded man's condition has changed for the worse recently: NO. the field marshal has led the courageous troops to victory: NO. silverware and plates have been made germfree: NO.

the queen was wearing a new hat: NO. unknown person is accused of having tipped over several gravestones: NO. the actor swooned while onstage: NO. a moist lip was the motive for the murder: NO. the bones were laid to rest in complete silence: NO. workers at that time were living in inhuman conditions: NO. two nations are entering into a nonaggression pact: NO. the newspaper did not appear yesterday: NO. the moon moved between sun and earth precisely according to calculations: NO. the leader went on foot: NO.

the first-class carriages can be found in the forward part of the train: NO. the mushrooms are no longer as poisonous once they have been cooked: NO. the family constitutes the germinal cell of the state: NO. the newspaper will be twice its usual size due to a special occasion: NO. everyone can eat his fill nowadays: NO. the trains go only as far as the border: NO. even the toughest cop goes soft at the sight of the empress: NO. the girl decorates the table with a rose: NO. due to constantly rising wages we find ourselves forced to announce a small price increase: NO. the king remains silent: NO. english is spoken here: NO. the farmer's sister is in the woods: NO. knives forks scissors and matches are not for little children: NO. the bomb comes from the east: NO. what's right must remain right: NO. our rooms are air-conditioned: NO. the father is working in the field: NO. whoever refuses to listen must be made to feel: NO.

the price includes breakfast: NO. you have entered a restricted area: NO. the train will presumably arrive a few minutes late: NO. we thank you for your visit: NO. illegible requests will be denied: NO. enjoyed in moderate quantities, alcohol is not harmful: NO. have you renewed your driver's license: NO. keep back, police regulations: NO. the missing-persons bureau of the red cross is looking for the following missing persons: NO. a high reward has been placed on the culprit's head: NO. the last row must stay empty: NO. everyone is waiting for the game-ending whistle: NO. belated protests won't be accepted: NO. please set the volume so that the noise will be confined to your room: NO. follow me unobtrusively please: NO. we wish you bon voyage: NO. there should be a death penalty for stealing food from little children: NO. show your hands: NO. green is good for your eyes: NO. the monarch is eager for reforms: NO. give me your i.d.: NO. anyone found on the street after dark will be shot: NO.

beyond this point only at your own risk: NO. keep it warm: NO. tear off here: NO. delete what is inapplicable: NO. enter in back: NO. don't eat for two hours: NO. show your tickets automatically: NO. push in the glass: NO. don't disturb: NO. use the service entrance: NO. read the directions: NO. print in capitals: NO. pull in your head: NO. hold children by the hand: NO. keep the receipt: NO. turn the key twice: NO. don't lose your head: NO. stay calm: NO. don't move the accident victim: NO. don't use spit as a spot remover: NO. be ready to show your i.d. cards: NO. go on: NO. don't fold: NO. wipe your shoes: NO. transfer: NO. make room: NO. apply the tourniquet above the wound: NO. buy now: NO. NO. raise your arm: NO. wait for the official signal: NO. close the doors: NO. protect against sunlight: NO.

in the name of the republic: NO. in one part of yesterday's edition: NO. lunch from twelve to two: NO. a six-month guarantee: NO. the first door to the left: NO. danger, construction: NO. know your terror threshold: NO. hats checked free: NO. hunting season closed from march to september: NO. blood group o: NO. trainee wanted: NO. ocean view: NO. sentenced to death in absentia: NO. measurements 38, 24, 34: NO. before the treatment and after the treatment: NO. nonpotable water: NO. all credit cards accepted: NO. police checkpoint within five thousand yards: NO. because of unprecedented demand: NO. not on saturdays: NO. an unknown victim: NO. next teller please: NO. two to three teaspoonfuls a day: NO. danger: NO. no dining car: NO. from our catalogue: NO. the fifty-second week!: NO. wet paint: NO. open all day today: NO. no cartoons due to the unusual length of the feature: NO. extra: NO. moved, address unknown: NO. only on weekdays: NO. against asthma attacks: NO. platform one: NO. addressee unknown: NO. one-way street: NO. insect repellent: NO. no more war: NO. reserved for women and children: NO. in the tenth round: NO. volunteers step forward: NO. in case of emergency: NO. to the turnpike: NO. towelettes twenty-five cents: NO. this establishment is being struck: NO. freedom for: NO. the penalty is increased by one sleepless night a month plus solitary confinement in complete darkness on the anniversary of the crime: NO.

lights out!: NO. enter!: NO. softly!: NO. thanks!: NO. present!: NO. heads up!: NO. to everyone!: NO. first name!: NO. beginning today!: NO. next!: NO. watch out!: NO. after, you, please!:

NO. profession!: NO. never!: NO. unfortunately!: NO. to the showers!: NO. wanted!: NO. until further notice!: NO. by the neck!: NO. hand it over!: NO. shut the door!: NO. undress!: NO. as of now!: NO. down!: NO. go on!: NO. sit!: NO. back!: NO. inri!: NO. bravo!: NO. hands up!: NO. eyes closed!: NO. smoke!: NO. into the corner!: NO. psst!: NO. aha!: NO. lie!: NO. hands on the table!: NO. up against the wall!: NO. no ifs, ands or buts!: NO. neither forward nor backward!: NO. yes!: NO. no delay!: NO. stretch out!: NO. no stopping!: NO. stop!: NO. fire!: NO. I'm drowning!: NO. ah!: NO. ouch!: NO. no!: NO. hello!: NO. holy!: NO. holy holy holy!: NO. over here!: NO. shut up!: NO. hot!: NO. air!: NO. hiss!: NO. water!: NO. away!: NO. emergency!: NO. never again!: NO. mortal danger!: NO. alarm!: NO. red!: NO. heil!: NO. light!: NO. behind!: NO. don't!: NO. there!: NO. here!: NO. upstairs!: NO. go!: NO. NO. NO:
help?: YES!
help?: YES!
help?: YES!

helYESpYEShelYESpYEShelYESpYEShelYESpYEShelYESpYEShelp

help

Translated by Michael Roloff

My Foot My Tutor

What, I say, my foot my tutor?
—SHAKESPEARE, *The Tempest*

The curtain opens.

It is a sunny day.

In the back of the stage we see, as the stage backdrop, the façade of a farmhouse.

The stage is not deep.

The left side of the stage, from our vantage point, shows a view of a cornfield.

The right side of the stage, from our vantage point, is formed by a view of a large beetfield.

Birds are circling above both fields.

In front of the farmhouse we see a peculiar, longish object and ask ourselves what it might represent.

A rubber coat, black, covers the object partially; yet it does not fit like a glove, and so we cannot recognize what the object represents onstage.

To the right of the picture of the farmhouse door, from our vantage point, we notice a wooden block with a hatchet in it in front of a window; or rather, a large piece of wood is lying on the block, which is not quite level on the ground, and a hatchet is sticking in the piece of wood. Round about the chopping block we notice many pieces of chopped wood, and also, of course, chips and splinters, strewn about the stage floor.

On the chopping block, next to the large piece of wood with the hatchet sticking in it, we notice a cat: while the curtain opens the cat probably raises its head and subsequently does what it usually does, so that we recognize: the cat represents what it does.

Upon first glance, we have seen someone sitting next to the chopping block, on a stool: a figure.

Now, after having briefly taken in the other features of the stage, we turn back to this figure sitting on a stool in the sunshine in front of the picture of the house.

He—the figure is that of a male—is dressed in rural garb: that is, he is wearing blue coveralls over his pants; his shoes are heavy; on top, the person is wearing only an undershirt.

No tattoos are visible on his arms.

The person wears no covering on his head.

The sun is shining.

It is probably not necessary to mention explicitly that the person squatting on the stool in front of the picture of the house is wearing a mask. This mask covers half of his face— the upper part, that is—and is immobile. It represents a face which, moreover, evinces an expression of considerable glee, within limits, of course.

The figure on the stage is young—some recognize that this figure probably represents the ward.

The ward has his legs stretched out in front of him.

We see that he is wearing hobnail boots.

The ward is holding the underside of his right knee with his left hand; the right leg, in contrast to the left, is slightly bent.

We see that the ward is leaning with his back against the backdrop representing the house wall.

In his right hand the figure is holding a rather large yellow apple. Now that the curtain has opened and is open, the figure brings the apple to his mouth.

The ward bites into the apple, as if no one were watching.

The apple does not crunch especially, as if no one were listening.

The picture as a whole exudes something of the quality of what one might call profound peacefulness.

The ward eats the apple, as if no one were watching.

(If you make a point to watch, apples are often eaten with a good deal of affectation.)

The figure thus consumes the apple, not particularly slowly, not particularly quickly.

The cat does what it does. If it should decide to leave the stage, no one should stop it from doing so.

If at first we paid too much attention to the figure, we now have sufficient time to inspect the other objects and areas (see above).

Can one gather from the manner in which the ward consumes the apple that he enjoys dependent status? Actually not.

Because we have been looking so intently, we have almost overlooked that the figure has already finished eating the apple. Nothing unusual has occurred during this process, the figure has no unusual way of consuming apples, perhaps a few seeds have fallen on the floor; chickens are not in evidence.

Now it's the second apple's turn.

To accomplish this, the ward stretches out his right leg completely, and with his left hand reaches under the coveralls into the right pocket of his pants. Obviously he is not making out too well.

He couldn't reach into the pocket with his right hand, however, since he would have to lean back to do so but sits too near the wall to be able to lean back as far as he would have to.

He slides forward with the stool and leans back against the picture of the wall: no, the upper and lower parts of his body are still at too much of an angle for his hand to be able to do what it wants to do.

The pause is noticeable.

The ward stands up and while he stands reaches into his pants pocket and easily extracts the apple.

While still in the process of sitting down, he bites into the apple.

With his bottom the ward shoves the stool closer to the wall of the house again and assumes a similar, though not precisely the same, position as the initial one; the cat moves or does not move, the ward eats.

From behind the cornfield backdrop—from our vantage point, the left—a second figure emerges, the warden, judging from all visible evidence: rubber boots covered with mud up to the knee, gray work pants, a checkered shirt (white & blue) with rolled-up sleeves, tattoos on his arms, an open collar, a mask covering the upper half of his face, a hat with a pheasant feather stuck in it, an insignia on the hat, a carpenter's pencil behind his ear, a very big pumpkin in front of his stomach.

Now that the warden has entered the stage, we see that the backdrop representing the cornfield consists of many small movable parts which are falling back into their original positions . . . the cornfield is calming down, the birds are again circling on one and the same spot.

The warden sees the ward.

The warden steps up close and takes a look at the ward.

The ward is quietly eating his apple.

The warden's watching the ward drags on.

Gradually, as we watch, the eating of the apple also begins to drag on.

The longer the warden watches the ward, the more the eating of the apple is drawn out.

When the warden has stared down the ward, the latter stops eating the apple.

The pumpkin which the warden is holding in front of his stomach is, as we see, a real pumpkin.

But we hardly notice this any more, for after the warden has outstared the ward and the ward has simultaneously ceased eating his apple, which is now lying oddly half-eaten in the ward's hand, the stage is already becoming gradually dark. The scene is finished.

A new scene now begins in the dark, we can hear it. What we hear is a loud, prerecorded breathing that is piped in over a loudspeaker. After a period of silence the loud breathing suddenly sets in, and it continues neither evenly louder nor softer but constantly wavering back and forth within its pre-scribed decibel range, in such a manner that we are made to think: now it will get louder and louder and become the loudest possible breathing, but at this point it suddenly becomes quite soft again, and we think: now the breathing is about to stop altogether, when it suddenly becomes loud again, and in fact far louder than what we consider natural breathing. It is "like" the strongly amplified breathing of an old man, but not quite; on the other hand, it is "like" the strongly amplified breathing of a wild animal that has been cornered, but not quite, either; it is "voracious," "frightened," "ominous," but not quite; at times it seems to signify some-one's "death throes" to us, but somehow it doesn't either because it appears to change location constantly. In the Italian spy film *The Chief Sends His Best Man* (with Stewart Granger and Peter van Eyck, directed by Sergio Sollima) there is a sequence in which an apartment—which someone has entered and in which he has found his dead friend—suddenly becomes dark; after a few moments of quiet the aforementioned breathing suddenly becomes audible all over the room, and for such a long time and so intensively that the intruder, in his desperation, starts shooting and jumps up from behind his chair, whereupon he is shot and the lights are turned on—a young man stands above him, a small tape recorder in his hand, which he now switches off, whereupon the "hideous" breathing stops: that is the kind of breathing that is meant here, without the same consequences, of course—as suddenly as it started, it stops again after a certain time.

We are sitting pretty much in the dark; judging from the noises coming from that direction, the stage is being rearranged.

While it is gradually becoming completely dark, we hear music, a succession of chords piped in very much at random, with the pauses between them varying in length. Occasionally several chords follow each other in quick succession.

The chords are taken from the tune "Colors for Susan" from *I Feel Like I'm Fixin' to Die* (Vanguard VSD 70266) by Country Joe and the Fish. The piece only lasts five minutes and fifty-seven seconds, so it's repeated over and over during the course of events, except for the very end of the tune, which is reserved for the end of the events.

Onstage, ward and warden are in the process of rearranging the stage: what was inside before is now turned inside out.

If the stage is of the revolving kind, this process is managed by turning the stage 180 degrees.

If the stage is not of the revolving kind, ward and warden simply turn the backdrops of the cornfield, beetfield, and house façade so that the backs of the backdrops now represent the inside walls of the house.

We look out through the back window, behind which the birds are circling.

Lacking a revolving stage, ward and warden take the objects that stood in front of the house (the object under the rubber coat, etc.) to the back of the stage, and now, as it becomes bright again, they bring the furnishings for the house onstage.

This is what is required for the play: a rather large table, two chairs, an electric hot plate, a coffee grinder, an assortment of bottles, glasses, cups, saucers, and plates (on the floor in back), an oil lamp, a rubber hose, a bootjack, a newspaper which sticks in the crack of the door.

On a nail on the door hangs a bullwhip; on the same nail there also hangs a pair of scissors.

We see a large monthly calendar hanging on what is, from our vantage point, the right wall of the room.

But so that we can see all of this, the following has transpired in the meantime: the warden lit a match in the dark and turned up the oil lamp. As we already know from many other plays, the entire stage gradually becomes bright when someone lights an oil lamp: the same happens here.

Now that the stage is brightly lit—let us not forget to listen to the music, which becomes neither softer nor louder—we see it in the following condition: it now represents the room of a house. But this room is still empty, except for the paper in the crack of the door, the objects on the door, and the calendar.

We see ward and warden, who come onstage from the left and right sides respectively, distribute the aforementioned objects throughout the room: each brings in a chair, then the table is brought onstage by the two of them, then comes the warden with the rubber hose, which he drags across the stage before dropping it, then comes the ward with the bottles and plates, then the warden with the glasses—unhurriedly but not ceremonially either—just as though we weren't watching; circus workers would go about it differently. No evincing of satisfaction, no contemplation of work well done, no moving to the music.

They both sit down, the ward almost first but he stops midway and the warden is seated, then the ward sits down too.

They both make themselves comfortable.

The music is pleasant.

The warden extends his legs under the table.

The ward also extends his legs under the table and comes to a halt when he touches the warden's feet; then, after a pause, the ward slowly withdraws his legs; the warden does not withdraw his.

The ward sits there. What to do with his legs?

Quiet, music.

The ward puts his feet on the front crosspiece of his own chair, and to accomplish this he uses his body to shove the chair back, producing the customary sound; the warden doesn't let himself be disturbed, he replies by taking off his hat and placing it on the table.

Quiet, music.

The ward slowly looks around the room, around, up, and also down, but avoids grazing the warden with his eyes, makes an about-face, so to speak, whenever he is just about to look at the warden: this is repeated so often that it loses its psychological significance.

The warden watches the ward.

The ward stands up, takes an apple from his pants pocket underneath the coveralls, and puts it beside the hat.

The warden lowers his gaze to the apple.

The ward starts gazing around the room again. What is there to see in the room?

Suddenly, as if he senses a trap, the warden cocks his head.

The ward, caught by the warden's gaze, stops looking around.

Mutual staring at each other, gazing, mutual looking through each other, mutual looking away. Each one looks at the other's ear.

The ward places both feet on the floor simultaneously; we can hear it.

The warden looks at the ward's ear.

The ward gets up carefully, softly.

The warden looks at him, at his ear.

The ward, aware only of himself, goes to the door, his steps, careful at first, becoming progressively louder as he approaches it.

The warden follows him with his eyes.

The ward bends down and pulls the newspaper out of the crack in the door.

The warden does not follow the ward with his eyes but keeps them fixed on the door: what's hanging on the door?

The ward straightens up, goes back to the table with the paper under his arm, walking progressively more carefully again, once by the table walking almost soundlessly; while underway he uses his free hand to take the paper from under his arm and holds it neatly in his hand by the time he stands before the table.

The warden gazes at the door.

The ward neatly places the paper beside the hat and the apple.

The warden lowers his head; in the pause between the movements we hear a louder chord.

The ward sits down without making a sound, sits the way he did before; the next chord is suddenly softer.

The warden unfolds the paper completely.

He reads. He folds the paper together to the size of one page. He pretends to read that page. He reads so that it is almost a pleasure to watch him reading.

The ward, while seated, pulls, with a good deal of effort, a tiny book out of his pants pocket, the same pants from which he produced the apples, and also reads and is no less pleasant to look at.

The warden folds the newspaper page in half and goes on reading.

The ward pulls a pencil out of his pants pocket, a carpenter's pencil like the warden's, only smaller; he uses it to mark in the book while reading.

The warden goes on folding the paper.

The ward no longer marks in his book but crosses something out.

The warden goes on folding as best he can.

The ward is obviously starting to draw in the little book.

The warden folds.

The ward exceeds the margins of the book while drawing and begins to draw on the palm of his hand.

The warden: see above.

The ward draws on the back of his hand.

The warden is gradually forced to start crumpling the paper, but we don't actually notice the transition from folding to crumpling.

The ward draws on his forearm; what he draws doesn't necessarily have to resemble the warden's tattoos.

The warden is obviously no longer reading or folding but is vigorously crumpling.

Both figures are vigorously occupied, one with drawing, the other with crumpling.

The warden completes the crumpling process and the paper is now a tight ball.

The ward is still drawing.

The warden is quiet, the ball of paper in his fist; he looks at his opposite, who is drawing.

The ward is drawing; the longer his opposite gazes at him, the more slowly he draws.

Then, instead of drawing, he merely scratches himself with the pencil and finally turns it around and scratches his arm with the other end; then he pushes the pencil into his arm without moving it. Then he stops doing this and slowly places the pencil next to the hat on the table; he quickly pulls his hand away and places it, slowly, on the forearm with the drawing on it.

The warden places his fist with the crumpled paper on the table and leaves it there.

The ward starts looking around the room once more, up, down, to the side, down along his legs.

The warden unclenches the fist holding the paper ball and places his hand next to it on the table; the paper ball slowly expands.

The music, noticeably louder now, is pleasant.

A period without movement—though that is not to say that the figures become graven images—now follows, unobtrusively introducing the next sequence.

During the period without movement we just listen to the music. Now the music becomes nearly inaudible, just as the main theme may disappear almost entirely during certain sections of a film.

We see the warden slowly place his forearms on the table.

In reply to this movement, the ward places his hands on the table, fingertips pointing at the warden.

The warden, without looking at the ward, slowly places his head on his forearms, on his hands, actually, and in such a way that his mouth and nose are placed on the backs of his hands, with his eyes looking across them.

Thereupon the ward slowly lowers his head toward the table until his head is hanging between his arms at the height of the table. After pausing briefly in this position and at this level, the ward lowers his head even further, down between his outstretched arms, which he has to bend now, until his head almost touches his knees: the ward remains in that position.

The warden draws his head toward himself until it lies, not with his mouth and nose, but with his forehead on his hands.

The ward spreads his knees and sticks his head deeper down between his bent arms and spread knees.

The warden pulls his hands out from under his head and now lies with his bare face, that is, with his bare mask, on the table.

(All these movements, although they occur very slowly, are not ceremonial.)

The ward lets his arms drop from the table but leaves his head hanging between his knees at the previous level.

The warden, while keeping his face in the previous position, uses his body to push the chair as far away from the table as possible, while still keeping his face on the table, his body slipping from the chair.

The ward, if possible, clenches his knees together above his head or against it.

Both of them are completely quiet onstage, as if no one were watching.

We hear the music somewhat more distinctly.

Some time passes; it has already passed.

The objects are in their places, here and there.

The warden stands up, without our noticing the in-between movements; he stands there, he represents standing, nothing else.

What will the ward do now?

Some time passes; we wait.

Now the ward sits up, without our particularly noticing the in-between movements.

What is the warden doing? He walks about the stage and represents walking.

The ward gets up; he stands there.

The warden runs; the ward begins to walk.

The warden leaps; the ward begins to . . .

The warden climbs up on a chair and is now standing on it; the ward does not leap but stops in his tracks and stands there.

The warden climbs on the table; the ward climbs on the chair.

The warden takes the other chair and puts it on the table and climbs on the chair on the table; the ward—how could it be otherwise?—climbs on the table.

The warden grabs on to a rope hanging down and hangs there; the ward climbs on the chair on the table.

The warden is hanging quietly, dangling a little, and the ward is quietly standing, high on the chair.

The warden lets himself drop. He lands with bent knees, then gradually straightens up to his full length.

The ward quickly climbs off the chair onto the table, from the table down onto the other chair, from this chair down onto the floor, and while doing so also takes the chair on the table down with him, putting it back in its old place and squatting down almost simultaneously.

All of this transpires so rapidly that if we wanted to count, we could hardly count further than one.

The warden slowly squats down.

The ward sits on the floor.

The warden slowly sits down also.

As soon as the warden sits down, the ward quickly lies down on the floor.

The warden slowly, ever so slowly, lies down on his back also, and makes himself comfortable.

As soon as the warden is lying on his back, the ward quickly rolls over and lies on his stomach.

The warden, emphasizing each of his movements with the sound it produces, also rolls over on his stomach, slowly.

As best he can, the ward now bends all his extremities together. We see him diminishing everywhere and becoming smaller. But he wasn't an inflated balloon before, was he? It appears that he was. The ward becomes smaller and smaller, and flatter, the stage becomes increasingly dark. The warden stays on his stomach as we last saw him, the stage is now dark, we hear the isolated chords.

The stage becomes bright.

We see that the two figures are again seated at the table in their previous positions.

The warden gets up, goes to the bootjack, takes off his boots in a completely professional manner, without exaggerating, as if no one were watching. He kicks each boot across the stage with one kick.

The ward gets up, goes where the boots are lying, and puts them next to each other beside the door.

One after the other, warden and ward go back to their places.

A brief pause.

The warden rolls his woolen socks from his feet and flings them, bunched up, across the stage, one here, the other there, without any evidence of nasty motives, just as if no one were watching.

The ward gets up, finds the socks, straightens them out, pulls them right side out, and places them as nicely as possible across the boots. Then he returns to the table and sits down.

The warden gets up, goes to the door, takes the scissors off the nail, and returns with the scissors to the table.

After sitting down, he places his naked foot on the side crosspiece of the chair and cuts his toenails.

We know the sounds.

He behaves as if we were not really watching.

He cuts his toenails so slowly and for such a long time that it no longer seems funny.

When he is finally done he places the scissors on his knees.

After some time the ward gets up and walks about the stage, picking up the clipped-off toenails and putting them in the palm of one hand.

He does this so slowly that it, too, is no longer a laughing matter.

When the ward finally straightens up and returns to the table, the warden takes the scissors from his knees and now begins to clip his fingernails.

The ward turns around and goes to the calendar hanging on the right-hand wall.

The warden cuts and the ward tears off a sheet from the calendar.

The warden cuts and . . .

The warden cuts and . . .

It is a slow process, without rhythm; it takes the warden a different amount of time to cut off each nail, and the ward needs a different amount of time to tear off each sheet from the calendar; the noises of the snipping and tearing overlap, are not necessarily successive, sometimes occur simultaneously; the calendar sheets flutter to the floor.

Now the calendar has been completely shorn: all we can see of it is the rather large empty cardboard backing left hanging on the wall.

But the warden is still cutting his fingernails, and the ward is standing inactively by the wall, his face half to the wall.

The music, which becomes more distinct, is so pleasant that the noise the scissors make hardly affects us.

And now that the stage is becoming dark the noise stops at once.

It becomes bright.

The two persons are sitting in their initial positions at the table, quietly, each by himself.

The warden gets up, goes to the hot plate. He takes the tea-kettle from behind the row of bottles and puts one end of the rubber hose into the kettle.

The warden exits, returns immediately.

We hear water running into the kettle.

The warden exits and returns at once.

He takes the hose out of the kettle, lets it drop. He puts the cover on the kettle and puts the kettle on the hot plate.

The warden drags the rubber hose onstage.

As the hose is apparently very long, he has to drag for quite a long time. Finally the warden drags the entire hose onstage.

Nothing funny happens.

He winds the hose in an orderly manner over hand and elbow, goes to the table, and places the rolled-up hose with the other objects on the table. He resumes his position.

Quietly, contemplating each other, the two figures squat onstage.

Gradually we begin to hear the water simmering in the kettle.

The noises we hear are those that are produced when water
```
   "        "     "     "    "    "       "    "      "         "       "
   "        "     "     "    "    "       "    "      "         "       "
```
is heated.
```
   "     "
   "     "
```

The ward gets up, fetches the coffee grinder, sits down, makes himself comfortable on the chair, clasps the coffee grinder between his knees and starts to grind. We can hear the grinding . . .

The ward is grinding, apparently unaware of anything
```
   "    "    "      "              "           "     "      "
   "    "    "      "              "           "     "      "
   "    "    "      "              "           "     "      "
   "    "    "      "              "           "     "      "
   "    "    "      "              "           "     "      "
```
else . . .
```
   "
   "
   "
   "
   "
```

The teakettle whistles . . .
```
   "        "         "
   "        "         "
```

The ward gradually stops grinding . . .
```
   "    "         "         "       "
   "    "         "         "       "
   "    "         "         "       "
```

Now the stopper is probably blown off the kettle, so that it becomes quiet again.

The music sets in at the appropriate moment, when the stage once more becomes dark.

On the bright stage we see the two persons at the table, the hot plate having of course been turned off in the meantime.

The warden gets up and goes offstage.

But he returns quite soon, a frying pan with glowing incense in one hand, a big piece of white chalk in the other.

We smell the incense and also see clouds of incense.

The warden goes to the door and starts writing something on the top of the door.

The moment he puts chalk to wood, the ward turns toward him on the chair; the ward reaches into his pants and throws something at the warden . . . it must be something very light because the warden does not stop his very slow writing, which looks almost like drawing.

The ward makes himself comfortable on his chair and throws again, unhurriedly.

The warden writes; the ward throws.

We see that the ward's projectiles are sticking to the warden's shirt: yes, they are thistles.

While the warden is slowly writing, the ward occasionally throws a thistle at him, yet without expressing anything with the manner in which he throws it.

We hear the music and smell the incense.

The warden's back is slowly but surely covered with a cluster of thistles while he writes.

He writes slowly down along the door:

K + M + B
K + M + B
K + M + B
K + M + B
,,   ,,   ,,
,,   ,,   ,,
,,   ,,   ,,
,,   ,,   ,,

The ward now takes the thistles out of his fist and throws them with the other hand.

The warden, while writing, takes the bullwhip from the door.

Now he steps back.

The ward happens to be throwing again.

The warden turns around as though accidentally, not quickly; at the same time, the ward throws a thistle, which hits the warden's chest (or not). The warden is standing there by himself; the ward throws the remaining thistles at the warden.

The warden is holding the pan with the incense in front of him. The longer the warden holds the pan, the longer the intervals between the ward's throws.

Meanwhile, it gradually becomes dark once again, and the music . . . (see above)

The two figures are sitting on the stage, which is bright again; they are sitting at the table, each one by himself.

They are sitting, each one by himself.

  ,,   ,,   ,,   ,,   ,, ,,   ,,

  ,,   ,,   ,,   ,,   ,, ,,   ,,

  ,,   ,,   ,,   ,,   ,, ,,   ,,

  ,,   ,,   ,,   ,,   ,, ,,   ,,

All at once we notice there is blood running from the ward's nose. The blood trickles out of his nose, across his mouth, over his chin, out of his nose . . .

The warden is sitting there by himself, the ward doesn't budge from the spot, doesn't budge from the spot . . .

Gradually it becomes dark again on the stage.

Once we can see again, both of them are sitting in their positions at the table.

The ward gets up and stands against the rear wall, with his back to us.

The warden gets up, goes to the ward, grabs him by the shoulder, without expressing anything (that is, not violently), and turns him around.

The warden, after a pause, changes the position of his hands and turns the ward around once more.

The turning around gradually turns into turning around and turning around, now into turning around pure and simple.

The warden turns the ward with ease, almost as though he were thinking of something else, and the ward turns easily, also as though he were thinking of something else.

Without transition, without either of them staggering, we suddenly see the warden standing by the bottles and plates.

The ward has been standing still for some time before we really notice that he is standing still.

The warden has already bent down and while bending down throws a bottle toward the ward: the ward shows how he would like to catch but can't—the bottle falls on the floor and does what it does.

As one can imagine, it goes on like this: Bending down, the warden throws bottles, plates, and glasses toward the ward, but the ward, although apparently making an effort, lets all the objects fall on the floor, and the objects either break or they don't.

This process also lacks a regular rhythm: they wait now and then, then the warden throws once more, then the ward misses again . . .

Suddenly, even before the collection of bottles has been disposed of—amid the nicest possible throwing and breaking—the ward catches an object, as if by accident.

We are startled.

At the same moment the stage becomes dark, abruptly.

And again it becomes bright, and both of them are sitting at the table. The warden gets up and goes where? Apparently he doesn't know where he should go.

No, he doesn't want to go to the calendar.

He turns around, turns around, is turning around.

The ward gets up and walks after him; he shows how he shares the warden's indecision and imitates the warden's gestures, his leg movements as well as his indecisive arm movements, although the imitation need not be a complete aping.

They almost collide when the warden suddenly changes direction—he is probably avoiding the pieces of the broken bottles and plates; more than once the ward steps on the warden's heels. They continue moving about the stage, pretending to have a goal which, however, they never reach, because they always give it up just before they are about to reach it.

Suddenly the warden is by the door, is already going out, reaches for the outside door handle to shut the door behind him—the ward seizes the door handle on the inside, wants to follow the warden, but the warden pulls without letup.

The ward pulls in the other direction.

The warden, by giving one hard pull, pulls the door shut behind him and in front of the ward, who has been pulled along by the violent pull.

The ward stands briefly in front of the door, his hand around the handle, then his hand merely touching the handle.

The ward lets his hand drop.

The warden is outside; it is quiet.

The ward gets down on his knees, without falling down on them, however, and is already crawling out the door, quickly: we see now that the door has an extra outlet, as if for a dog.

Once the ward is outside, the stage slowly becomes dark.

By now we have become accustomed to the music.

The pause is longer this time, for the scenery is being turned inside out.

A revolving stage needs only to revolve.

Otherwise, the scenery is turned around in the dark.

It becomes bright: it is a rainy day.

Warden and ward set up the objects on the stage: the

large, longish object, covered by the black raincoat, which they have to bring onstage together, the stool, beets, melons, pumpkins.

When everything has been distributed on the stage, the ward sits down on the stool while the warden stands next to the mysterious object.

Without an actual beginning the play has begun again: the warden takes the rubber coat off the object, so that we see that it is a beet-cutting machine.

The warden puts on the raincoat (he is still barefoot) and, to test the machine, lets the cutting knife drop down several times without, however, cutting any beets.

The ward gets up and walks to the machine. The warden bends down for a beet, shoves it into the machine, and pulls down the cutting knife with one brief, effortless movement, as he indicates with a movement: the beet falls down, its top shorn off.

The warden repeats the process in detail, demonstrating: another beet falls down.

The ward watches, not completely motionless, but without moving very much.

The warden repeats the process.

The ward fetches a beet but makes many superfluous movements and detours; we can hear his hobnail boots on the floor as well as the bare feet of the warden, who now goes to the side and straightens up.

The ward raises the cutting knife, shoves the beet up to its top into the machine, and hacks off the top.

The warden steps up to him, stands beside him, steps back again . . .

The ward goes and fetches a few beets and puts them into place . . .

The warden steps up to him and stands there.

The cat suddenly slinks out of the house.

The ward's next attempt to cut off the top of a beet is so feeble that the beet does not fall on the floor at once.

The warden stands there watching him.

With the next attempt, the beet falls on the floor.

The cat does what it does.

The warden stands there.

The ward has problems with the beet again: he makes one attempt to sever its top, a second one, and then, without looking at the warden, who is starting to walk about the stage once more in his bare feet, a third attempt; then, after a certain time, when the warden is standing next to him again and is watching him, once more; then, later—it is already becoming darker on stage—a fifth time (the warden is starting to walk again); then—it is already quite dark (is the warden standing by the machine?)—finally once more, and now —we can't bear watching it any more—once again, and we don't hear the sound of anything falling on the floor; thereupon it is quiet onstage, for quite some time.

After it has been quiet onstage for some time we hear, quite softly at first, a breathing that becomes increasingly louder. We recognize it. It becomes louder, that is, larger and larger—a death rattle? A very intense inhaling? Or only a bellows? Or a huge animal?

It becomes steadily louder.

Gradually it becomes too large for the house.

Is it here, is it over there?

Suddenly it is quiet.

After a long time it becomes bright again.

The house, the cornfield, the beetfield.

We see neither the cat, nor the warden, nor the ward; not even the beet-cutting machine remains onstage—except for the three backdrops, it is bare.

Now someone enters from the right: it is the ward.

He is carrying a small tub in front of him, and wound about his upper body is a rubber hose.

He is no longer wearing his coveralls.

The tub is placed on the floor, the hose is unrolled.

One end of the hose is placed in the tub; the ward takes the other end offstage, straightening the hose in the process.

We hear the water running into the tub for some time.

Then the ward returns, a sack of sand in one arm.

He puts the sack next to the tub.

He reaches into the sack with his hand.

He straightens up and lets a handful of sand fall into the tub, without letting the sand slip between his fingers first.

He again reaches into the sack and, standing, lets a handful of sand fall into the water.

He again reaches into the sack and, standing, lets a handful of sand fall into the water, nonchalantly, irregularly, unceremoniously.

He again reaches into the sack and, standing, lets a handful of sand fall into the water.

Now we hear the isolated chords again.

The ward reaches into the sack and, standing, lets a hand-
The ward reaches into the sack and, standing, lets a hand-
The ward reaches into the sack and, standing, lets a hand-

„   „   „   „   „   „   „   „   „   „   „
„   „   „   „   „   „   „   „   „   „   „
„   „   „   „   „   „   „   „   „   „   „
„   „   „   „   „   „   „   „   „   „   „

ful of sand fall into the water.
ful of sand fall into the water.
ful of sand fall into the water.

„   „   „   „   „   „   „
„   „   „   „   „   „   „
„   „   „   „   „   „   „
„   „   „   „   „   „   „

We hear both, the chords and the sand falling into the

„   „   „   „   „   „   „   „   „   „   „
„   „   „   „   „   „   „   „   „   „   „
„   „   „   „   „   „   „   „   „   „   „
„   „   „   „   „   „   „   „   „   „   „
„   „   „   „   „   „   „   „   „   „   „

water, as the stage gradually becomes dark.

   „   „ „   „   „   „   „

   „   „ „   „   „   „   „

   „   „ „   „   „   „   „

   „   „ „   „   „   „   „

   „   „ „   „   „   „   „

The curtain closes.

Translated by Michael Roloff

Quodlibet

Translator's note

More than any of Handke's plays to date, Quodlibet (*written in 1969, between* Kaspar *and* The Ride Across Lake Constance) *requires fairly extensive adaptation to an American linguistic, cultural, and historical environment. Why this is necessary is made apparent by the play itself. What finally surprised me, though, was the comparative ease with which indigenously German allusions—allusions to the various manifestations, public and private, of fascism—can be replaced by American equivalents. In further adaptations, which a cast may want to make, it would be worthwhile to consult the invectives at the end of Handke's* Offending the Audience (Publikumsbeschimpfung) *simply to see how "not to overdo it." This translation is meant as a basic model for American productions.*

M.R.

The curtain rises. On the bare stage, one by one, talking quietly to each other, appear the figures of the "world theater": a general in uniform, a bishop in his vestments, a dean in his gown; a Maltese knight in the coat of his order; a member of a German student corps with his little cap and sash; a Chicago gangster with his fedora and pin-striped double-breasted suit, a politician with two heavily armed CIA bodyguards; a dance-contest couple—he in a dark suit and white turtleneck sweater, she in a short, pert dress; a grande dame in a long evening gown, carrying a fan; another female figure in a pants suit, a poodle on the leash.

These figures come on stage in no particular order, separately or in pairs, arm in arm or not. Chatting, they slowly walk about the stage, step here and there, laugh softly at some remark or other, walk on again, not that one hears them walking of course. Each chats with the others at some point; every so often one of them stands apart alone as though struck suddenly by some thought before starting a new conversation; only the bodyguards take no part in the conversations; they nod to each other occasionally, that's all; otherwise they keep peering away from the figures on stage into the surrounding area, once up into the rigging loft, then—this without bending down—into the prompter's box, then into the vault of the theater as though up into the fifth tier of an opera house—at any event, never at the audience itself: the audience does not exist for the figures on the stage. One notices that all the figures briefly come to a complete stop, but the next moment one or two are walking again. At moments the general conversation almost lapses into complete silence; there are also moments during which only the rustling of garments on the floor is audible, whereafter the conversation resumes more vociferously and insistently than before.

The figures walk about making almost no sound, lost in themselves, stand still, are still, chat: that's actually all there is to it. It's entirely up to the actors what they want to say. They can talk about what they've just read in the papers, what they've experienced that day, what they want to experience, about what just occurred to them, or about something that gives the impression of having just occurred to them . . . a few times one thinks one hears them speaking a foreign language, probably French: C'est très simple, Monsieur.—Ah merci . . . oh! ma coiffure! . . . Ah! Ce vent! . . . Cette pluie! . . . Or something of that kind, invariably uttered by the women. The audience of course strains to listen, but only occasionally gets a few words, or snatches of sentences.

Among the words and sentences that the audience does understand—besides the irrelevant and meaningless ones like "Do you understand?" "Not that I know," "Why not?" "As I said," "And you?"—are some which the audience merely thinks it understands. These are words and expressions which in the theater act like bugle calls: political expressions, expressions relating to sex, the anal sphere, violence. Of course the audience does not really hear the actual expressions but only similar ones; the latter are the signal for the former; the audience is bound to hear the right ones. For example, instead of *napalm* they mention *no palms* onstage; instead of *Hiroshima* they speak of a *hero sandwich*; instead of *cun-*

nilingus of cunning fingers; instead of *psychopath of bicycle path;* instead of *leathernecks* of *leather next;* instead of *Auschwitz* of *house wits;* instead of *dirty niggers* of *dirty knickers* . . . Or the actors use double-edged words in sentences with invariably harmless connotations, but in such quick succession that one listens to the ambiguous words instead of the sentences, for example: *thigh, prick, member, spread, panties, tear, pant, cancer, victim, fag, rag, paralysis, stroke, frag* . . . Many sentences, which appear to be quite harmless, are also uttered in quick succession; however, they contain words which, when they appear in clusters, begin to give the illusion of an allusion: A sentence with the words *tiger cage* ("I didn't want to put my tiger in the cage but the cops insisted.") is followed by a sentence containing the word *gook* ("I wasn't completely satisfied until I had wiped the gook off the wall."), which is followed by a sentence with the word *waste* ("Sad to say, but we had to waste a lot of . . . time"), which is followed by a sentence containing the words *anti-personnel weapon* ("Anti-Americanism is a weapon I personally refuse to use."), which is followed by a sentence with the word *infrastructure* ("The infrastructure of the organization, if I may say so, consists of living bodies, all you have to do is count them"), which of course also contains the words *body count* in slightly different form, and which is followed by a sentence containing a distorted form of the words *Tonkin Gulf & Saigon* ("Tom's kinfolk made a resolution not to take the Gulf Line steamer to *Saigon*.") and finally a sentence containing the proper name *My Lai*, also in distorted form because of the proximity of the event ("As the old bastard of an Irishman used to say to me about Dora: 'She was me last lay before me prostate operation, and she was me very best lay.'").

The *hit* turns out to be a *two-run hit*, the *beating* is a *beating around the bush*, the *bomb* turns out to be *what a bomb this play was*, the *smashed brain on the stone* turns into *mashed potatoes alone*, where someone *spread blood* it turns out that the *old beer-belly actually sweated Bud*; when *shot* is mentioned it only refers to a *shot* of *whiskey*; and what *shot through his head* were only *thoughts*; "Shot through the head!"—"Shot through the head?"—"Yes, thoughts shot through my head." *Syphilis* is *Sisyphus* & *the clap* is a *thunderclap* & a *dildo* becomes *dill does it too.*

"Cashes in!"—"Cashes in pretty good!"—"The cops?"—"By the cops!"—"Cashed in?"

". . . broken!"—"with grief . . ."—"The neck?"—"A bottle!"—". . . the neck!"—"Broken . . ."—". . . and stuck the finger in . . ."—"Good!"—"Cut off!"—"What kind of head?"—"The conversation?"—"What?"—"He's one good head shorter."—"Off."—"What kind of head?"—"Good, good."

". . . three, four:"—"One, two, three—go!"—"One, two, three, four, five, six, seven . . ."—"One, two, three, four, five, six, seven (*pause*) eight (*pause*) nine (*pause*) ten—finished!" "Once, once more, a third time, four times, five times, and once more . . ."—"And then it was already getting bright outside . . ."—"Twenty-one, twenty-two—it's uncanny, uncanny."—"And then I stopped counting . . ."

"Corpses in quiet waters . . ."—"Oh, what a pretty title"—"Like an O?"—". . . laying their eggs there."—"Like *Story of O?*"—"As *though* it were nothing . . ."—"Shame!"—". . . 'and didn't say a single word!' "—"What a beautiful title!"—"Oh!"—". . . the carps lay their eggs in quiet waters . . ."—"In Lake Erie?"—"Shame! shame! and shame once more!"—"Let's say it was nothing!"—"According to the Geneva convention, o.k.?"

"The project died . . ."—" 'Dying' is a typo, actually it should say 'dried'!"—"Of fear?"—"A projectile with a cross-notch at the tip . . ."—"Quietly!"—"Died?"—"Very quietly!"—"I'm dying."—"What was the name of that bar?"—"Dum-Dum!"—"Of laughter?"—"I can't go on!"—"Blood?"—"Into the blood!"—"As for me, he died!"—"Died for all of us . . ."—"Quiet!"—"Psst!"—"Silence!"—(*silence*)—"An angel walked through the room!"—"Oh, Harlem . . . !"—"Yes."

—"Unforgettable those tulip fields!"—"Haarlem . . ."—
"Yeasz . . ."

". . . shaking with fear!"—"Pardon the question: 'Shaking with fear'?"—Someone else in the background: ". . . shake well before use!"—"Excuse me!"

". . . could be seen from far away: fucked the cows . . ." —"Fucked?"—"Forgot the cows, John Wayne. I believe, I forgot the name of the film."—Someone farther away: "Knocked out her teeth!"—"Who knocked her up?"—And someone even farther away: "Knocked them down with bombs."

Continuing at once: "Rammed a rod up his ass!"—Louder: "Ramrods have passed."—Quite comprehensible but not too loud, recited negligently like verse: ". . . rambling through the brambles of glass . . . / . . . roaring through the riptide of grass . . ." To his partner: "Do you still remember?" The partner lowers his or her head, smiles, and walks on: "Whether W. C. Fields slipping freely . . ." The first one, more softly: "Sipping."—Even more softly: "What simpering?" The sound of someone becoming louder emanates from an altogether different spot: ". . . . chalice of sorrow . . ." Now the first of the two partners walks on smiling. And on: "And a bit of spit on the fly which . . ." The lady with the fan in the background.—"Yes, the tits of my girl Friday." One thereupon thinks one hears one of the two partners saying.—"No, a dog that bit off my clitoris(?) . . ."

While stepping-slowly-forward: ". . . and I tasted . . ." Correcting himself while approaching: ". . . which tasted me . . ."—". . . tasted the soft inside of a . . . cyst . . ."— In front by the footlights, humming elatedly with lowered head: ". . . a foretaste of heaven . . ."—A character who is just walking past the lady with the fan says: "Tested me to the utmost," and one thinks one can still hear the lady with the fan's partner say—one can't really make out who is speaking— while the two are edging into the background: ". . . cash his cut . . . taste buds . . . spit and polish . . . soft insides got sick . . . fucked watery corpses at Easter . . ." while all around on the stage many other characters are walking around chatting, though more softly, and smiling.

Then they recount: " 'Cold,' he said, 'cold, completely cold.' "—" 'Ice,' as she used to say then."—" 'Like a glance out of a ranch house in Nebraska,' they told us."—" 'Where the train got stuck in the snow,' she wrote back to me."—" 'Indescribably white!' she exclaimed."—" 'No!' he screamed."— " 'Light, nothing but light!' she squealed like a pig on a spit."—"He cabled: 'In the chest-high snow where the two, who had become snowblind in the meantime, were surrounded by St. Bernards . . .' "—"And I replied: 'And what are you?' "—" 'Put in cold storage,' I still understood, then the line went dead."—" 'A mouse?' I couldn't resist asking."— " 'For New Year's Eve in the fridge!' he wrote in so many words though the stamp allowed room for one more."—"The note said in Gothic script: 'Born dead . . .' "—" 'The ice pick already lodged in his head,' I read, 'he still bit his murderer's hand.' "—Someone then produces a poor imitation of the sound of "croaking," a chocking noise with the gums— *kch*—and his female partner emits a quick light laugh.

For a short while one hears the characters leave out one word in their sentences and sees them casting significant and conspiratorial glances at each other: "You remember how (*smirking and nodding of heads*) . . . used take lonely walks with his dog?"—"I don't need to tell you that . . . held different opinions on the matter."—"I often thought of . . . when I sat in my deck chair."—"When the radio announcer says . . . I drop everything at once."—"For days after . . . had squeezed my hand my whole body would break out in hives."—"I can't forget how . . . dangled on his suspenders on the hotel room door."—"It's unthinkable that . . . would have gone out on the street without his umbrella."—"What would have been different if . . . had succeeded in getting a hit at that time?"—"Not only when I sat on Plymouth Rock did I have to cry about what . . . told me about death."—"I often worry myself nearly to death whether Paraguay is really the right place for . . ."—"Usually one glance by a dark-eyed foreigner in an Indonesian restaurant is enough and I can't breathe any more and only see . . . (*outraged recollection*) in front of me—how he suddenly stepped out from behind the column toward (*melancholy recollection*) . . ."

Or they use the wrong instead of the correct word under the assumption that they understand each other anyway. "One should herd them together and then—'treat them to a good meal!' " (*Smirking and gentle laughter.*)—"Go after them—'and slap them on the shoulder!' "—". . . because his 'shirt tail' hung out of his 'door' . . ."—". . . When she came up to me and told me that I could 'visit' her."—"All I had to do was 'smile' at him and blood began pouring from his nose."—". . . grabbed between his legs to help him 'get upstairs.' "—"His dentures fell out of his mouth even before I'd 'said a single word.' "—"The 'slight draft' when we entered the room was enough for him to catch his death of cold."—"Up on the platform 'I kissed him on the forehead,' so that he suddenly lost his balance."—"Drove him, 'drove him out of his wits.' "—"Got caught in the fan belt and—'woke up!' "—"I sent him a 'get-well card' registered mail and the man thanked me and dropped dead!"—"He aimed at—'progress and change!' "—". . . I tried putting the 'cookie' in his mouth!!"—"Across the barbed wire—'into the soft moss of the Okefenokee, . . .' "—"Cut a 'piece of bread' off for him!"—". . . will give her a teaspoonful of 'cinnamon,' 'to taste!' "—". . . so that these bastards will let her 'come.' "

Then one of the figures in the background tells a joke of which again one only hears the key words, such as "then he said," "the second time," "again nothing"; all the other characters except maybe for two or three and the bodyguards are assembled around the narrator at this point. They listen quietly and finally, each in his own way, smile quietly to themselves, scream with laughter, shake their heads in puzzlement, inhale deeply (one of them perhaps out of turn), and then continue to circle about the stage.

From the conversations one has also managed to pick out with increasing frequency sentences which a figure speaks with a slightly raised though not overly excited voice: sentences from the repertoire of politicians when they are forced to defend themselves against catcalls from the audience, and which are useful to them as defense against interjections from the audience but are employed even when there are no interjections. For example: "Anyone who shouts shows that he doesn't have anything to say." "I would die to defend your right to speak, but would you do the same for me?" "What you don't have in your head gets stuck in your throat." "Your parents don't seem to have brought you up to let other people finish what they are saying." "Take one look at these characters and you get a permanent itch in your trigger finger." "I won't take back one iota of what I said." "Our economic accomplishments give us the right not to be constantly reminded of the past." "Oh, I see the lady is a gentleman!" "Those people with their caveman feelings and their Stone Age laughter want to set back our discussion by a thousand years." "You don't even notice how useful you are to us!" "Long hair and dirty fingernails are no proof that you're right!" "Just take one look at them, that's what they all look like!" "All I say is: Stalin, Stalin, Stalin!" "There's only one weapon against radicalism, and that's the vote." "They should first condemn the torture of the prisoners in North Vietnam." "We are controlled by the iron law of history." Plus what other set rejoinders of this kind exist [campaign speeches contain some rich pickings.—Trans.]. Not that the characters exaggerate them or address them directly to the audience or someone particular in the audience—rather, they speak them as asides, almost in a monologue, quietly and with finality, while they walk about the stage in their state of extraordinarily malicious and melancholy solitude. If someone fails to recognize this, and wants to join them on the stage, the bodyguards gently and without hurting him or her should lead the person off. To let the person remain on stage would only be a show of disdain.

While all characters begin to busy themselves more and more with themselves—stroking their hair, forehead, cheeks, lips; cracking their joints, picking lint off their clothes, slapping themselves on their arms, stomach, neck, and throat, stopping occasionally to tug at their earlobes—one also hears fragments of monologues which keep breaking off or become inaudible, as though the speakers were ashamed of what they were saying: ". . . I decided to join the company as a silent partner . . ."—"Last night I dreamed of Arizona . . ."— ". . . I saw the people's faces change color in the completely sold-out stadium . . ."—". . . I wrapped the boa around my neck and winked at him like Jane . . ."—". . . I suddenly saw a landscape as quiet and dreamlike as the transparent wing of a butterfly . . ."—". . . I kept the option of taking further steps . . ."—". . . at that time when I slipped off a pile of logs in my dream . . ."—(*A lady slowly raises her dress, beneath which she is completely naked, and slowly lets it fall again.*) ". . . and I heard my baby sister sighing in the kitchen . . ."—As though remembering, a few characters shake their heads one after the other and walk on. And while they are already walking again one of them says: ". . . while I was about to fall asleep I saw two hanged men dangling from one noose . . ."

For some time, that is, at least until the audience begins to pay attention, the characters move quietly around the stage like this, with their belt buckles, their collar patches, brooches and rings glinting in the muted light. Then while the chatter gradually subsides, because more and more characters stop talking, one can still hear one of them say: "What, when the pain becomes unbearable you want to simply waste them like animals?" And another replies: "Yes, should animals be any worse off than human beings?" And a little later someone else: "Yes, if I'd defended him at the

trial, he might even have been able to wriggle his way out."
And after the chatter has even further subsided—only now
does one notice how heavily made up the characters are—the
lady with the fan says softly but distinctly: "Even before he
touched me I began to cream." And the two bodyguards, who
stand quite far away, exchange obscene gestures. One pushes
his thumb out between the middle and index finger of a
closed fist; the other immediately replies by making a fist
and whopping quickly up and down on the other fist. From
the lady with the lapdog one hears, already as a memory, a
pretty, long-drawn-out "Ahh . . ." and at this point it becomes gradually dark on stage and the curtain drops.

Translated by Michael Roloff

The Ride Across Lake
Constance

It's a winter night. A man rides across Lake Constance without sparing his horse. When he arrives on the other side, his friends congratulate him profusely, saying: "What a surprise! How did you ever make it! The ice is no more than an inch thick!" The rider hesitates briefly, then drops off his horse. He is instantly dead.

M.R.

Characters

WOMAN WITH WHITE SCARF

EMIL JANNINGS

HEINRICH GEORGE

ELISABETH BERGNER

ERICH VON STROHEIM

HENNY PORTEN

ALICE AND ELLEN KESSLER

A DOLL

To avoid character designations such as "Actor A," "Actor B," "Actress C," and so on, for reading and other purposes the characters in the play have been given the names of well-known actors.

When the play is staged, the characters should bear the names of the actors playing the roles: the actors are and play themselves at one and the same time.

"Are You Dreaming or Are You Speaking?"

The stage is large. It displays a section of an even larger room. The background is formed by the back wall of this room; the wall is covered by a brownish-green tapestry with a barely perceptible pattern. Along the back wall two parts of a staircase lead down from the right and left and meet in the center of the wall, where they form a single set of wide stairs, of which a number of steps lead forward into the room. The audience therefore sees persons walking down the stairs first in profile, then from the front. In the wall beneath the right and left parts of the stairway are two barely visible tapestry doors. The staircase has a delicately curved, slender bannister. The floor of the room is covered with an unobtrusive carpet whose color matches the tapestry; a wine-red runner leads down the staircase steps.

Most of the furnishings in the room are covered with drop-cloths; these are extremely white. In the center of the room, not precisely center of course, rather almost downstage, stands a large dark table, partially covered by a lace table-cloth; on it are an ashtray, a cigar box, a teapot or coffee pot covered with an embroidered cozy, a longish cutlery case, also of embroidered cloth, and two candlesticks sheathed in protective covers. To the right and left and behind the table

*stand three fauteuils with white dropcloths; next to and be-
hind them are an easy chair and a straight chair, dropcloths
over both. In front of one of the fauteuils stands a stool upholstered the same and the same height as the fauteuil that
may serve as a footrest; a smaller footstool stands in front
of the second fauteuil; the third fauteuil stands by itself. To
the right of the table, a few steps away, stands a small bar,
not covered, with several bottles whose forms indicate their
respective contents. To the left of the table, a few steps
away, stands a newspaper table, not covered either, with a
few bulky magazines, some of which are still rolled up; on
top is a record player with a record on it. Looking further to
the left and right behind the newspaper table and bar one
sees two sofas, also concealed by white dropcloths. To the
left side of the left sofa is a brown-stained chest, with several
drawers; on it a small statue covered with a white paper bag.
On the right side of the right sofa leans a guitar in a bag
embroidered like the tea cozy. Beneath the sections of the
staircase hang two pictures on the wall concealed behind
white sheets. Downstage to the extreme right, in line with
the table, is a Japanese screen of the kind one usually sets up
in front of beds. It is small and has three panels; two of
them are slightly pushed together, the third is open and
visible to the audience. The screen has the same pattern and
color as the back wall.*

*All objects are in such a position that it would be difficult
to imagine them standing elsewhere; it is as though they
could not bear being moved ever so slightly. Everything
appears as though rooted to the spot, not only the objects
themselves but also the distances and empty spaces between
them.*

The light is that of early morning.

*After the curtain has opened, two portieres to the right
and left of the proscenium are revealed, as portieres to a*
chambre séparée.

A WOMAN, *her hair wrapped in a* WHITE SCARF, *moves*

quickly but not hastily among the objects with a vacuum cleaner. She is in blackface. The vacuum cleaner, which was turned on the moment the curtain began to open, makes a more or less steady noise.

On a fauteuil beside the table, his legs on the appropriate footstool, sits EMIL JANNINGS, *his eyes closed. He is quite fat. His boots stand next to the stool. He is wearing red silk socks, black pants, a light-colored shirt, open at the collar. He seems costumed although only hints of a costume are visible: rather long frills on the sleeves of the silk shirt, a wine-red silk sash around his stomach.*

He is heavily made up, the eyebrows are painted. On the right hand, whose nails are lacquered black, he wears several large rings.

He has not moved since the curtain opened, and the WOMAN *has nearly completed her work. Pushing the vacuum cleaner back and forth near the newspaper table with one hand, she turns on the record player with the other.*

However, one hears only a few isolated sounds; the vacuum cleaner is too noisy.

She takes the cleaner to the back wall and turns it off so that the music becomes audible: "The Garden Is Open" by T. Kupferberg. She pulls the plug out of the socket, rolls it up on the machine, and places the machine behind the tapestry door.

While the record continues to play, she walks from object to object and takes off the dropcloths, except those on the paintings and on the statue. Although she moves fairly slowly, her work is proceeding quite rapidly; at least, one barely notices it. She pulls the cover from under EMIL JANNINGS *with a single movement and walks off to the left while the record is still playing.*

Then nothing moves onstage for a while except for the record.

The record player turns itself off, and after a moment JANNINGS *slowly opens his eyes.*

JANNINGS

(*With a cracked voice*) As I said—(*He clears his throat once and repeats in a firm voice.*) As I said. (*Pause.*) A bad moment. (*Someone behind the screen with a cracked voice:* "Why?" *He clears his throat twice; the second time he does so he steps out from behind the screen, repeats then in a firm voice:* "Why?" *It is* HEINRICH GEORGE, *quite fat, his clothes also suggesting a costume, with braids trimming his jacket and with lace-up shoes. He stands there.* JANNINGS *has turned his head away slightly.*) It's over already.

GEORGE

(*Takes a step toward* JANNINGS *and collapses. As he slowly rises again*) My foot has fallen asleep.

JANNINGS

(*Reaches for the cigar box. He lifts it but cannot hold on to it so that it falls to the floor.*) So has my hand. (GEORGE *carefully walks up to* JANNINGS, *stops next to him. Both of them glance at each other for the first time, then look away again.* GEORGE *leans against the edge of the table, now sits down on it. The cigar box is lying on the floor between them. Both look at it.* JANNINGS *turns his head toward* GEORGE. GEORGE *slides off the table.* JANNINGS *points at the cigar box.* GEORGE *misunderstands the gesture and looks as if there was something to see on the box.* JANNINGS *agrees to the misunderstanding and now points as if he really wanted to point out something.*) That blue sky you see on the label, my dear fellow, it really exists there.

GEORGE

(*Bends down to the cigar box, takes it, looks at it.*) You're right! (*He puts the box back on the floor and straightens up.*)

JANNINGS
You're standing . . .

GEORGE
(*Interrupts him.*) I can also sit down. (*He sits down in the fauteuil with the smaller footstool and makes himself comfortable.*) What did you want to say?

JANNINGS
"You're standing just now: would you be kind enough to hand me the cigar box from the floor?"

(*Pause.*)

GEORGE
You were dreaming?

JANNINGS
When the nights were especially long, in winter.

GEORGE
You must be dreaming.

JANNINGS
Once, on a winter evening, I was sitting with someone in a restaurant. As I said, it was evening, we sat by the window and were talking about a corpse; about a suicide who had leaped into the river. Outside, it rained. We held the menus in our hands. "Don't look to the right!" (GEORGE *quickly looks to the left, then to the right.*) shouted the person opposite me. I looked to the right: but there was no corpse. Besides, my friend had meant I should not look on the right page of the menu because that was where the prices were marked. (*Pause.*) How do you like the story?

GEORGE
So it was only a story?

(*Pause.*)

JANNINGS
When one tells it, it seems like that to oneself.

GEORGE
Like a story? (JANNINGS *nods. Pause. Then he slowly shakes his head.*) So you're wrong after all. Then it's true what you told me?

JANNINGS
I'm just wondering.

(*Pause.*)

GEORGE
And how did it go on?

JANNINGS
We ordered kidneys flambé.

GEORGE
And you got them?

JANNINGS
Of course.

GEORGE
And asked for the check and got it?

JANNINGS
Naturally.

GEORGE
And asked for the coats and got them?

JANNINGS
Why the coats?

GEORGE
Because it was a winter evening.

JANNINGS
(*Relieved*) Of course.

GEORGE
And then?

JANNINGS
We went home.

(*Both laugh with relief. Pause.*)

GEORGE
Only one thing I don't understand. Of what significance is
the winter evening to the story? There was no need to mention it, was there? (JANNINGS *closes his eyes and thinks.*)
Are you asleep?

JANNINGS
(*Opens his eyes.*) Yes, that was it! You asked me whether I
was dreaming and I told you how long I sleep during winter
nights and that I then begin to dream toward morning, and
as an example I wanted to tell you a dream that might occur
during a winter night.

GEORGE
Might occur?

JANNINGS
I invented the dream. As I said, it was only an example. The
sort of thing that goes through one's head . . . As I said—
a story . . .

GEORGE
But the kidneys flambé?

JANNINGS
Have you ever had kidneys flambé?

GEORGE
No. Not that I know.

JANNINGS
If you don't know, then you haven't had them.

GEORGE
No.

JANNINGS
You're disagreeing with me?

GEORGE
Yes, that is: no. That is: yes, I agree with you.

JANNINGS
In other words, when you mention kidneys flambé, you talk about something you know nothing about.

GEORGE
That's what I wanted to say.

JANNINGS
And about something one doesn't know, one shouldn't talk, isn't that so?

GEORGE
Indeed.

(JANNINGS *makes the appropriate gesture with his hand, turning up his palm in the process.* GEORGE *stares at it, and under the impression that* GEORGE *has found something on the palm* JANNINGS *leaves it like that. The hand now looks as*

*if it is waiting for something; say, for the cigar box. After what
has been said just now the hand has the effect of an invita-
tion, so that* GEORGE *bends down and puts the box in* JAN-
NINGS's *hand.*

A brief pause, as if JANNINGS *had expected something else.
Then he takes the box with his other hand and puts it on
his knee. He looks at his hand, which is still extended.*)

JANNINGS
That's not what I meant to say with that. It just seemed to
me that you had noticed something on my hand. (*He opens
the box top with his other hand and offers the box to* GEORGE,
who looks inside.) Take one.

(GEORGE *quickly takes a cigar.* JANNINGS *takes one too.*
GEORGE *takes the box from* JANNINGS *and puts it back on the
table. Each lights his own cigar. Both lean back and smoke.*)

GEORGE
Haven't you noticed anything?

JANNINGS
Speak. (*Pause.*) Please, go ahead and speak.

GEORGE
Didn't you notice how silly everything suddenly became when
we began to talk about kidneys flambé? No, not so much
suddenly as gradually, the more often we mentioned the
kidneys flambé. Kidneys flambé, kidneys flambé, kidneys
flambé! And didn't it strike you why the kidneys flambé
gradually made everything so hair-raisingly silly?

(*Pause.*)

JANNINGS
Speak.

GEORGE

Because we spoke about something that wasn't visible at the time. Because we mentioned something that wasn't there at the time! And do you know how I happened to notice this?

(*Pause.*)

JANNINGS

Speak.

GEORGE

When you made that motion with your hand two minutes ago—

JANNINGS

(*Interrupts him.*) Two minutes have passed since then?

GEORGE

It may also have been earlier. In any case—what was I about to say?

JANNINGS

When I made that motion with my hand . . .

GEORGE

When you made that motion with your hand, I suddenly noticed the rings on your fingers and thought to myself: ah, rings! Look at that, rings! Indeed: rings! And then I saw the rings again, and when what I thought and what I saw coincided so magically, I was so happy for a moment that I couldn't help but put the cigar box in your hand. And only then I noticed how ridiculous I had seemed to myself speaking all that time about kidneys flambé! I wasn't even myself any more, my hairs rose on end when I spoke about them. And only when I saw the rings and thought: ah, the rings!

and then cast a *second* glance at the rings, then it seemed to me that I was no longer confused.

JANNINGS
And I felt you were handing me the box voluntarily.

GEORGE
Do you understand me?

JANNINGS
From a human point of view, yes.

GEORGE
Take a look around. (*They take a look around the room.*) Car. (*They hesitate a little, continue looking around the room.*) Cattle prod. (*They hesitate, continue looking around the room.*) Bloodhounds. (*They look around the room, hesitate.*) Swollen bellies. (*Only* JANNINGS *looks around the room, hesitates.*) Trigger button.

JANNINGS
(*Quickly looks at* GEORGE.) You're right, let's talk about my rings!

GEORGE
There's nothing left to say about the rings. (JANNINGS *remains silent.*) It's meaningless.

JANNINGS
I?

GEORGE
Your rings.

JANNINGS
And?

GEORGE

(*Irritated*) "And" what?

JANNINGS

(*Irritated*) And? (*Pause. The pause becomes increasingly laden with animosity. Both smoke. When they notice that they are simultaneously drawing on their cigars, they stop and hold their breath. When one of them wants to blow out smoke, he notices that the other is just about to exhale and he hesitates; only then does he emit the smoke from his mouth.* JANNINGS *suddenly, in a very friendly manner*) And if they were *your* rings?

GEORGE

(*Suddenly looks at him in a very friendly manner.*) But they are yours! (*Pause. They hardly move. The pause becomes increasingly laden with animosity.*) But they're *your* rings? (*Suddenly* JANNINGS *pulls the rings from his fingers.* GEORGE *understands, bends forward, spreading his fingers apart.* JANNINGS *places the rings on the table.* GEORGE *slips them easily and as though routinely, almost without looking, on his fingers. He regards his hand.*) As if they were made for me! (*Pause.*) As if they had always belonged to me! (*Pause.*) They *were* made for me! (*Pause.*) And they *have* always belonged to me! (*He holds the rings up to the light so that they sparkle. He caresses them and touches each individually with his lips. He plays: points with the ringless hand at something, then points with the ringed hand at the same thing; places the ringless hand on his heart, then places the ringed hand on it; waves someone toward him with a ringless finger, then with a ringed one; threatens someone with a naked finger, then with a ringed one. He is intoxicated by the idea of ownership.*) I can't even imagine my hand without rings any more! I can't it me—I can't myself—me myself —myself me—I can't myself me—I simply can't imagine myself without rings any more! Can you imagine me without rings? (JANNINGS *makes no reply.* GEORGE *sets out to make a speech.*) Expensive rings! Just as you, who are round, know no beginning and no end, in the same way—(*He hesitates and begins once more.*) And just as you transform the light that strikes you and are changed yourselves by the light, in the same way—(*He hesitates. Pause.*) In any cause—you elicit similes from me. Since I own you, you mean something to me. (*Pause.*) To wear rings on every finger—what does that mean? Wealth? Early death? To take care while climbing ladders? Job problems? Watch out, danger!?

(*Pause.*)

JANNINGS
I've never dreamed of rings so far.

GEORGE
Because you never owned any.

(*Pause.*)

JANNINGS
On the contrary, because I owned some. (*Pause.*) And they never elicit similes from me.

GEORGE
Because they weren't enough for you.

(*Pause.*)

JANNINGS
On the contrary, because they were enough for me.

(*Pause.*)

GEORGE
Just as . . .

JANNINGS
What do you mean, "Just—as"?

GEORGE
Bide your time! (*He begins once more.*) Just as there are born losers, born troublemakers, and born criminals . . .

JANNINGS
Who says they exist?

GEORGE
I do!

JANNINGS
That doesn't prove anything.

(*Pause.*)

GEORGE
Have you ever heard people talk about a "born loser"?

JANNINGS
Frequently.

GEORGE
And have you ever heard the expression "born troublemaker"?

JANNINGS
Indeed.

GEORGE
And the expression "born criminal"?

JANNINGS
Of course.

GEORGE
But the expression "a scurrying snake"—that you have heard
quite frequently?

JANNINGS
No, never.

GEORGE
And have you ever heard of a "fiery Eskimo"?

JANNINGS
Not that I know.

GEORGE
If you don't know it, then you haven't heard of it either. But
the expression "a flying ship"—that you have heard?

JANNINGS
At most in a fairy tale.

GEORGE
But scurrying snakes *exist?*

JANNINGS
Of course not.

GEORGE
But fiery Eskimos—they exist?

JANNINGS
I can't imagine it.

GEORGE
But flying ships exist?

JANNINGS
At most in a dream.

GEORGE
Not in reality?

JANNINGS
Not in reality.

(*Pause.*)

GEORGE
But born losers?

JANNINGS
Consequently, they do exist.

GEORGE
And born troublemakers?

JANNINGS
They exist.

GEORGE
And therefore there are born criminals?

JANNINGS
It's only logical.

GEORGE
As I wanted to say at the time . . .

JANNINGS
(*Interrupts him.*) "At the time"? Has it been that long already?

GEORGE

(*Hesitates; astonished*) Yes, that's odd! (*Then continues rapidly.*) Just as there are born losers, born troublemakers, and born criminals, there are (*He spreads his fingers.*) born owners. Most people as soon as they own something are not themselves any more. They lose their balance and become ridiculous. Estranged from themselves they begin to squint. Bed wetters who stand next to their bed in the morning. (The bed signifies their possession. Or perhaps their shame?) (*Brief moment of confusion, then he continues at once.*) I, on the other hand, am a born owner: only when I possess something do I become myself . . .

JANNINGS

(*Interrupts him.*) "Born owner"? I've never heard that expression.

(*Pause.*)

GEORGE

(*Suddenly*) "Life is a game"—you must have heard people say that? (JANNINGS *makes no reply, waits.*) And a game has winners and losers, right? (JANNINGS *makes no reply.*) And those who don't get anything are the losers, and those who can have everything are the winners, right? (JANNINGS *makes no reply, only bends forward, opens his mouth, but not to speak.*) And do you know the expression "born winner"?

(*Silence. Suddenly both burst out laughing and slap each other's thighs. While they are still doing so, a woman appears above left on the staircase. She is beautiful. She is wearing a long dress in which she moves as though it were carrying her. She has appeared noiselessly and has walked down a few steps. She stops in the middle of the left staircase, puts her hand on the bannister, and turns her head a little: it is* ELISABETH BERGNER. *Her hands are empty, no handbag.*)

She observes the strange scene beneath her with lowered eyelids: JANNINGS *and* GEORGE *are busy pulling each other's ears and patting each other's cheeks. She moves a few steps farther down and now remains standing, face forward, on the wide center staircase. With lowered eyelids she appears to observe the two below her:* JANNINGS *is just showing* GEORGE *the back of his hand;* GEORGE *replies by making a circle with his thumb and forefinger and then holding his hand in front of his face; and* JANNINGS *replies to this sign by holding both hands above his head, loosely clasping one wrist with thumb and forefinger of the other hand and letting the clasped hand circle about itself, whereupon both of them burst out laughing once again, and again start slapping each other's thighs, making exclamations such as* "Exactly!" "You guessed it!" *Then one of them slowly calms down while the other continues to slap his thighs.*

In the meantime, two other persons have appeared on the right section of the staircase; both of them have stopped at once and observed the strange scene below: a man and a woman. One can recognize them: ERICH VON STROHEIM *and* HENNY PORTEN. *He is impressive, wears a red dressing gown over a gray vest and pants as the only hint at a costume. She wears an evening dress with a velvet stole.*

As they appear, PORTEN *loudly claps her handbag shut and* VON STROHEIM *pulls up the zipper in back of her dress, then fastens his collar button:* "As I said . . ." *But it now becomes unclear how they belong together; they stand two steps apart.*

The noise of the handbag has made one of the two downstairs gradually quiet down. "Don't turn around!" *he says to the other.*

The other immediately turns around and sees the three persons standing on the staircase. "No corpse," *he says to the other.* "You can turn around: everyone is alive."

The other turns around, then he rubs his eyes fervently.

"Don't you believe me?" *the first one asks.*

"I just wasn't prepared for such a bright light," *he replies.* "I didn't know that it was so late already. We've lost all track of time with our talking!"

"We?" *the first one asks at once.*

"I," *answers the other.*

Pause.

"Yes, me too," *the first one says.*

PORTEN *is rocking back and forth on the stairway, plays with her stole; the others are rather quiet.*

PORTEN *slowly proceeds farther down the stairway, grazes* VON STROHEIM *with her stole, then exaggerates the way she steps around him.* VON STROHEIM *quickly overtakes her, stops with his back to her as if to block her path.* PORTEN *smooths down the back collar of his dressing gown, which was turned up, blows softly on his neck, and walks on. Where the two sections of the staircase join,* VON STROHEIM *stops next to* BERGNER *and bends over her neck from the back. She slowly turns around with lowered eyelids, puts her arms around his neck, leans her head against his chest.* PORTEN *has come closer, touches* BERGNER's *hip with the handbag.* BERGNER *turns her head toward her, frees herself from* VON STROHEIM, *with slow movements takes the handbag from* PORTEN *and dreamily hangs it over her own shoulder, and in the same manner offers her hand to* VON STROHEIM, *palm up. He suggests a kiss on the palm, then takes a step aside so that* POR-TEN, *who in the meantime has stepped behind him, now "takes her turn" and bends over the hand which* BERGNER *has turned over.* PORTEN *gives the incident a different interpretation by only looking at the hand over which she is bent. She straightens up, keeps the hand in hers, and guides it to* VON STROHEIM *as if she wanted to point out something on it to him.* VON STROHEIM *nods as though he saw it too. This nodding, however, gradually becomes a sign that he agrees to the following:* PORTEN *guides* BERGNER'S *hand under* VON STROHEIM'S *vest and moves it caressingly around,* BERGNER *suddenly withdraws the hand and lets it drop. But it is* PORTEN *who emits a brief scream. She makes a small curtsy in front of* BERGNER *and then suggests a bow in front of* VON STROHEIM. *Then she takes a step back, squints at one of the two—one doesn't know at whom—and proceeds to go down the few steps into the room.*

GEORGE *and* JANNINGS *have been the audience in the meantime. But when* PORTEN *begins to walk down, they become alert and begin to count simultaneously:* "One, two, three . . ." PORTEN *slowly descends into the room.* "Four, five, seven!" *She was just about to place her foot on the sixth step, now she hesitates as if she might fall, then runs back up the steps. She begins to walk down again.* "One, two, three, four, five, six, and seven!" *But there is also an eighth step and* PORTEN, *thinking she had reached level ground, stumbles, staggers into the room, gasps for air, and quickly runs back upstairs as if she had been repulsed. She snuggles up to* VON STROHEIM.

"Courage! Get up your courage!" *they call to her from below. They whistle the way one whistles to a dog.*

VON STROHEIM *puts his arm around her, supports her by the shoulder, proceeds to lead her slowly downstairs. Her eyes are closed.*

The two below have started counting again. "One, two, three, four, five, six, seven, eight, nine!" *At* "eight" VON STROHEIM *and* PORTEN *have safely arrived downstairs, but at* "nine" *they walk down one more step, one that does not exist. They bounce on the floor, go half down to their knees, stagger.* PORTEN *wants to run back but* VON STROHEIM, *who is also unsteady on his feet, leads her to a sofa. He eases her down, but while he is doing so she clutches him, feels with one hand for the sofa, and then lets herself gradually down.*

She slowly leans back and sits there with tightly closed eyes, immobile, while VON STROHEIM *walks step by step to the table where* JANNINGS *and* GEORGE *sit and watch. Hesitating after each movement, both hands propped up on it, he gradually sits down in the fauteuil without a footstool. He wants to lean back, stops, sits there quietly with open eyes. He blinks rapidly, with long pauses in between.*

The audience now looks up to BERGNER. *She stands there with lowered eyelids.* GEORGE *and* JANNINGS *tiptoe quickly to the stairs and, each holding a finger to the other's mouth, lie down parallel to the lowest step, one on his back, the other on his stomach.* BERGNER *comes down the stairs and steps over stomach and back on the floor. She is already on her way to the table. As* GEORGE *and* JANNINGS *get up and wipe the dust off each other's clothes, she has already settled in the easy chair, taken the cozy off the teapot, poured tea for herself, and, without looking up, brought the cup to her lips—as if she had done all that in one single movement.*

GEORGE *and* JANNINGS *walk back to the table, confused.*)

GEORGE
Once more: I offer you my fauteuil. (BERGNER *makes no reply.*) May I offer you my fauteuil?

BERGNER
(*As if asleep*) On the streets the insurmountable filth, the frost, the snowstorms, the immense distances . . .

JANNINGS
What did she say?

GEORGE
Nothing. She is dreaming. (*To* BERGNER, *as to someone who is talking in his sleep*) Who are you?

BERGNER

I only walked into the parlor to turn off the light and have
been lost without a trace ever since.

GEORGE
Who?

BERGNER

Watch out! the candlestick is falling! (JANNINGS *and* GEORGE
*turn around, but the candlestick stands motionless on the
table.* BERGNER *quickly opens her eyes; screams at once*) Who
are you? What do you want? Where am I? (*During these
questions she has quieted down again and finished them only
for form's sake. She gets up and sits down in one of the free
fauteuils, but leaps up again at once.*) It's still warm! (*She
tries the second fauteuil and gets up again at once.*) How
dare you offer me a chair that is still warm?

JANNINGS
I?

BERGNER
No, he. (*She points at* GEORGE.)

PORTEN
(*Sitting quietly in the rear on the sofa, has opened her eyes.*)
What snowstorms?

(VON STROHEIM *stops blinking his eyes and follows the
conversation.*)

BERGNER
(*To* GEORGE) Why don't you answer? (*To* JANNINGS) He
doesn't answer? (JANNINGS *stammers.*) Think before you
speak!

(*Pause.*)

JANNINGS
(*Fluently*) Perhaps he felt you didn't expect an answer to
your question.

BERGNER
Can't he answer for himself?

JANNINGS
I speak for him.

BERGNER
Are you more powerful than he is?

JANNINGS
Why? I mean, why do you ask?

BERGNER
Because you speak for him. (JANNINGS *is taken aback. He
looks at* GEORGE, *who returns the glance.* JANNINGS *stammers.
Pause.* BERGNER *quickly*) Does he please you? (JANNINGS
nods absentmindedly.) Naturally, as your friend he can't
help but please you.

JANNINGS
More powerful? Yes . . . Yes, why not? (*To* GEORGE) Right?
I speak for you, therefore you have to listen to what I say!
(GEORGE *nods playfully.*) You're not my friend! If someone
has something to say here, it's me! (*Pause.* JANNINGS *and*
GEORGE *begin to play.* JANNINGS *drops into the fauteuil and
stretches out his feet.*) The boots! (GEORGE *quickly steps up
to him, gets down on one knee, and puts on* JANNINGS's
boots.) The tea! (GEORGE *quickly pours into a cup; hands
him the cup.*) The sugar! (GEORGE *offers him the sugar bowl.*
JANNINGS *takes a piece with the sugar tongs and lets it drop
elegantly into the cup.*) A spoon! (GEORGE *hands him a
spoon. Both grin, are close to giggling.* JANNINGS *stirs once*

snappily with the spoon.) The newspaper! (GEORGE *is already by the newspaper table and back.*) My glasses!

GEORGE
(*Blurts out*) But you don't wear glasses!

JANNINGS
(*Snorts.*) The mustard! The hairbrush! The . . . (*He hesitates.*)

GEORGE
(*Assists him.*) The photo album! The pincers!

JANNINGS
(*With a surgeon's gesture*) The scalpel! The scissors!

GEORGE
A permanent—and make it snappy!

JANNINGS
(*Reaching blindly behind him with gestures of an auto mechanic.*) The pliers! The monkey wrench! The soldering iron!

GEORGE
Hand over all your money—and be quick about it, if you please!

JANNINGS
The sun!

GEORGE
(*Hesitates.*) Why the sun?

JANNINGS
(*Fatigued by the game*) The sun has come up.

GEORGE

(*Confused*) Why? I mean, why do you say that?

JANNINGS

(*Snaps at him.*) Those are *my* words! (*As if exhausted*) I don't know why.

GEORGE

(*Confused, but indifferent*) Your saying so doesn't change anything. (*The last words he has spoken to himself.*)

(*In fact, the dawn light did change gradually some time ago to a normal stage light.*
Finally one hears VON STROHEIM.)

VON STROHEIM

Wrong! Entirely wrong! (*He gets up quickly.* BERGNER *has turned toward him; whereas she previously had turned away from the others as if disappointed.*) I'll show you how it should be done!

(*Pause. All prepare to watch.*

VON STROHEIM *takes a slow look around as if he is about to pick out someone.* GEORGE *and* JANNINGS *draw in their heads when his glance passes them. Finally* VON STROHEIM *examines* PORTEN. *Since he has his back to the audience, the fact that he is looking at her can only be gleaned from her response to him. First she leans forward, sits upright. Then she rises like a sleepwalker, walks toward* VON STROHEIM, *stops in front of him. Standing before him, she wants to take off his dressing gown, but then steps behind him and take it off from behind; while doing so, she does not seem to touch him. She walks to the tapestry door behind which the vacuum cleaner is stored, hangs the coat inside, takes out a wine-red smoking jacket;*

back again behind VON STROHEIM, *she spreads it out and he*
slips into it; again they do not touch one another. GEORGE, *as*
spectator, coughs.)

JANNINGS
Psst!

(PORTEN *pulls* VON STROHEIM'*s cuffs from under his jacket*
sleeves. Pause. VON STROHEIM *now describes a quarter circle*
with his hand, signaling PORTEN *to stand in front of him. She*
obeys immediately and, in doing so, makes sure never to turn
her back to him. She stops in front of him. He beckons her
with his index finger to come closer. Pause.

JANNINGS, *eagerly watching, points with a similar circular*
movement of his hand at the cigar box. GEORGE, *also en-*
thralled, has noticed the movement out of the corner of his
eye and obeys blindly by handing JANNINGS *the box from the*
table, still watching the two. Then he realizes what he has
done and is quite startled. He looks toward JANNINGS. *They*
look at one another rather startled and immediately turn
back to the action.

VON STROHEIM *pulls* PORTEN *closer to him by the stole.*
Playfully he steps a little to the side so that PORTEN *is com-*
pletely visible too. He grabs her with his index finger under
the chin and lifts her face. Pause. He strokes the back of her
head. Pause. He pats her fondly on the shoulder. Pause. He
drums with two fingers on her cheek. Pause. He snaps his
fingers against her teeth. Pause. He pulls her lower eyelid
down with his finger. Pause. He gives her a pat on the behind
so that she goes half down on her knees. Pause. GEORGE
coughs.)

JANNINGS
Psst!

(VON STROHEIM *turns* PORTEN *around, so that she stands*
with her back to him and walks back a step. Pause. GEORGE

coughs. Still sitting, JANNINGS *gives him a kick.* GEORGE, *standing by the table, jerks forward a little; but* PORTEN, *as if she had been kicked, tumbles across the stage toward the sofa and remains lying in front of it. In fact,* VON STROHEIM *had already lifted his knee to administer a kick. Pause. Startled, they all look at each other. Pause.)*

BERGNER

It's nice to watch when something is beginning to function smoothly. It's like watching a sale: move after move. Here the goods, there the money! Here the money, there the goods! Or like listening to two people talking: first the question, then the reply. Someone holds out his hand, the other shakes it. How are you, I'm fine! How do you like him, I think he's okay! Someone gets up, you're already leaving? Someone sighs, and you pat him. Oh, that's beautiful!

(VON STROHEIM *slowly lowers his leg, turns around slightly dazed.* PORTEN *pulls herself up on the sofa and sits down, her face half turned away.*

GEORGE *sits down bewildered in the fauteuil.* JANNINGS *looks at the boot with which he kicked him. He pinches his leg and upper arm a few times.* GEORGE, *too, fiercely pinches his arm once.* BERGNER *sighs. She walks up to* VON STROHEIM, *then stops short. He comes toward her, then stops. She takes his hand, puts it on her breast. She caresses herself with his hand until he begins to caress her.* PORTEN *suddenly gets up and runs toward the table.* GEORGE, *who from her viewpoint is sitting behind the table, stands up unintentionally.* BERGNER *and* VON STROHEIM *let go of each other and watch.)*

GEORGE

(*Asks*) What would you like? (*The words slipped out.*)

PORTEN

(*Like a customer*) Do you carry gas pistols?

GEORGE
Gas pistols? You mean "tear-gas pistols"?

PORTEN
Aren't you the salesman? (GEORGE *makes no reply.*) You were
sitting behind the table and got up when I came in; you're the
salesman, aren't you?

GEORGE
(*Looks at* JANNINGS, *who signifies to him to agree with her.*)
The salesman? You mean I am "the salesman"? Well, why
shouldn't I be the salesman? I asked you, didn't I, "What
would you like?" What would you like? A weapon perhaps,
for the way home after dark?

PORTEN
A tear-gas pistol!

GEORGE
(*To* JANNINGS, *who sits as if he were the boss in his fauteuil.*)
Do we carry tear-gas pistols?

  (JANNINGS *pulls a small riding crop out of his boot and
hands it to* GEORGE, *who puts it on the table.* PORTEN *looks at
it without touching it.*)

JANNINGS
(*Sits with his face turned away from her.*) This riding crop
will do the trick too.

GEORGE
A riding crop like this will do the trick too.

PORTEN
I want *this* one.

JANNINGS
Is she our first customer today?

GEORGE
(*Translates.*) A customer like you should be treated like the
first customer of the day. It's yours!

PORTEN
(*Takes the crop.*) Is it a good one?

GEORGE
First-rate.

PORTEN
Can I believe you?

GEORGE
What reason would I have to trick you? (*She hands the crop
back to him, and he slashes through the air with it. One can
hear the sound. Then he slaps the crop on the table.*) Just
imagine the sound in the dark! (*He hands her the crop.*)

(PORTEN *repeats what he did, producing the same sounds.
The crop still in her hand, she pulls up her dress as far as the
hip and pulls a large note of stage money out of her garter
belt. She puts the note on the table and also places the crop
next to it.*

GEORGE, *astonished, hands the crop back to her, then takes
a few coins out of his pants pocket and puts them on the
table. While he is looking for banknotes in his other pockets,
PORTEN takes the coins; but when he continues to search,
she puts the coins back on the table.*

JANNINGS *gets up and flashes a few notes, which he counts
into her hand one by one. He closes her fingers one by one
over the notes; the last finger—it is the index finger—she
closes, very slowly, herself. It seems that she beckons him to*

*come to her. At the same time they look into each other's
eyes. Everyone is holding his breath.*

PORTEN *pushes the bills into her bodice; then slowly withdraws her hand, making it evident that the hand is now
empty; touches her upper lip with the tongue; and, gently
flipping the crop back and forth, looks so long at the two
salesmen that* GEORGE *shifts his weight from one leg to the
other and shouts indecently loud at* VON STROHEIM: "Do
you belong together?" VON STROHEIM *and* PORTEN *give each
other a fleeting glance, then look away. A second glance:
they look at each other as though for the first time.*)

VON STROHEIM
Can't one tell just by looking at us? (*He steps toward* PORTEN
*and grabs her around the waist, and she stops flipping the
crop.*)

GEORGE
I guess so, now.

PORTEN
(*To* GEORGE *and* JANNINGS) And how is it with you two? Do
you belong together?

(GEORGE *and* JANNINGS *look at each other, look away. The
second glance: they look at each other as though for the
first time.*)

GEORGE *and* JANNINGS
(*Simultaneously*) Yes, he belongs to me. (*To one another,*
GEORGE *softly,* JANNINGS *louder*) You belong to me—you
belong to me.

GEORGE
Why?

JANNINGS
Because it has always been like that.

GEORGE
Who says that?

JANNINGS
People in general.

GEORGE
And why do you tell me that only now?

JANNINGS
There was no need to tell you until now.

GEORGE
And now it has become necessary?

JANNINGS
(*Looks at his cold cigar.*) Yes. (*He points with the cigar at the box of matches lying on the footstool.* GEORGE *bends down, then he hesitates and straightens up again.*) There, you see how necessary it was. (GEORGE, *confused, thereupon hands him the matches, and* JANNINGS, *content, lights his cigar. He drops the match.*) You've lost something there.

(GEORGE *glances briefly at the match, looks away. The second glance: he picks up the match and puts it in the ashtray.*)

VON STROHEIM
(*Applauds by way of suggestion, but one hears no clapping.*) Much better already! Much better! Of course, if I were you . . .

PORTEN
Who's stopping you?

VON STROHEIM

Yes, who's stopping me? (*He takes a deep breath and assumes a pose.* (JANNINGS *takes the coins from the table and flings them into his face.* VON STROHEIM *shakes himself and comes to his senses. He speaks to* JANNINGS *and* GEORGE *as though teaching them something.*) You're still here?

JANNINGS

(*Repeating, but twice as loud*) You're still here?

VON STROHEIM

That's it! Exactly! That's how I would have done it! (*Pause.* VON STROHEIM *gives* JANNINGS *a sign to go on speaking. He prompts him.*) What do you want here?

JANNINGS

What do you want here?

VON STROHEIM

We just want to take a look around.

JANNINGS

This isn't an amusement park!

VON STROHEIM

Why don't you let *him* speak for himself!

(JANNINGS *nods to* GEORGE *and sits down on the fauteuil, his back to the others.*)

GEORGE

This is private property. (JANNINGS *nods.*) You're not in a restaurant. You have nothing to say here. Please talk to each other only in whispers. If you must intrude here, at least take off your hats. Didn't you see the felt slippers by the entrance? Look at me: I'm talking to you. You're not at home here, where you can put your feet on the table. What has the world come to that anybody can come in? Watch your step, man-traps and self-detonating charges have been set. Danger, rat poison. Don't touch anything. Beware of dog. Long, hard winter. Floods in spring, mud in the closets, no more cranes wake with their shrill screams in the meadows, no more June bugs buzz through the maple trees. (*Pause.*) It's terribly painful to be alive and alone at one and the same time.

(*Pause.*)

VON STROHEIM
He'll never learn it.

(*Pause.*)

GEORGE
It wasn't raining yet, but farther away one could hear it already raining . . .

(VON STROHEIM *turns away with* PORTEN *and walks around with her as if he wanted to inspect the furnishings. He wants to take out a magazine, but when he straightens up with it, it turns out that the magazine is chained to the table, like a telephone book, and he quickly puts it back. Then* PORTEN *wants to pick up the little statue covered with a paper bag, but it turns out that the statue is either screwed or glued to the chest of drawers. She pulls the bag from the statue: it is a multicolored painted dog sitting in an upright position. She touches it and it squeaks: it is made of rubber.* VON STROHEIM *joins her and pulls on one of the chest drawers. It will not open although he makes repeated attempts. Finally he tries a different drawer, which opens very easily.*)

VON STROHEIM
You see!

(*They leave the drawer open and continue their inspection tour. He takes off and drops the cover from the first picture: a seascape, not a rough sea, not a calm sea, no ships, only ocean and sky.*

Almost simultaneously PORTEN *has removed the cover from the second picture: a mirror without particular characteristics. She settles on the second, so far unused, sofa while* VON STROHEIM *returns from the bar with a bottle and two glasses. He sits down next to her and twists the bottle top but cannot open it. He quite casually blows into the glasses, and a cloud of dust swirls into his face. He casually puts the glasses and bottle aside. He looks at his hands, turns one palm up and down.*)

PORTEN
(*Suddenly seizes his hand.*) Watch out! (*Pause. She sees his hand.*) Oh, it's only your hand. I thought, an animal.

VON STROHEIM
Why don't you look at me?

PORTEN
I don't dare look at you closely because I'm afraid I might catch you at something! (*She looks at him.*)

(*Pause.* BERGNER *in the meantime has gone to the mirror and calmly viewed herself in it.*

GEORGE, *still standing, carefully wipes the cutlery on the table with a large red cloth he pulled out of his pocket and then places it—now and then he tries to stand it on end—on a second red cloth as if he were putting the cutlery on display. He and* JANNINGS *are spectators.*

PORTEN *has put her hand on* VON STROHEIM's *knee and is caressing her own hand with her other one.*)

VON STROHEIM

(*Moves his lips soundlessly, but every so often a word becomes audible.*) Snowplows . . . hedges . . . a dog portrait? (*At one point he presses down the intertwined fingers of both hands so that the joints crack.*)

(BERGNER *is combing herself, but with movements becoming increasingly more insecure. She does not know in which direction to comb while viewing herself in the mirror. With a small pair of scissors she wants to cut a strand of hair, holding it away from her head, but keeps missing until she finally lets go of the strand. She wants to put on makeup, pencils the eyebrows and the eyelines, puts rouge on her cheeks, powders her nose, puts on lipstick. But as she does this her movements become more and more shaky, and contradictory. She confuses the direction in which she wishes to draw the lines. She is mixed up. She wants to put the cosmetics back into the handbag but they fall to the floor. She walks away. She turns around, walks in the opposite direction, at the same time looking back over her shoulder, turns around again. She is totally confused, her face is badly made up. She walks in a direction where no one is and says:* "Help me!" *but with wrong gestures, hopping around. She bumps into things, bends forward to pick up things that physically lie behind her.*)

PORTEN

(*Calls to her.*) Open your eyes! Say something! Pull yourself together! (*But* BERGNER *does not turn her head toward her, instead to somewhere else.* PORTEN *gets up and walks up to her from behind.*) Don't be frightened.

BERGNER

(*Startled, looks up toward the stairs. She tries to point to the painting with the seascape but is unable to.*) It winked at me! It's winking at me!

(PORTEN *calms her down by caressing her and leading her around the room. Together they bend down for the coins and other things on the floor. At first* PORTEN *guides her hand, then* BERGNER *reaches for the things herself and also points at them correctly again. While doing this they talk to each other, and the longer they talk, the more sure of themselves and graceful they become.*)

PORTEN

Once when it rained I walked with an open umbrella across a wide, heavily traveled, street. When I had finally reached the other side, I caught myself closing the umbrella.

BERGNER

And once when I— Please, help me. (*She is still insecure.*)

PORTEN

(*Grabs her and wipes her face with the stole.*) Once when I bent over a bouquet of carnations while there was a great deal of noise around me, I couldn't smell anything at first.

BERGNER

Once while I wanted to put a tablecloth over . . . (*She cannot think of the word and becomes afraid again.*) Help me, please.

PORTEN

(*Speaks now very distinctly to set an example.*) Once I walked down a stairway and had such an urge to let myself fall that out of fear I began to run as soon as I had reached the bottom.

BERGNER

(*Breathes a sigh of relief.*) Once I wanted to put a tablecloth over a table, I was with my thoughts (*She neatly points to the picture.*) at the seashore and caught myself shaking the tablecloth as if wanting to wave with it.

(*They embrace, then dance around while they put the coins and cosmetics into the handbag. They talk and move more and more lightheartedly.*)

PORTEN
Why "caught"? Why not: "I saw myself," "I noticed"?

BERGNER
I saw myself! I noticed myself! I heard myself!

(*They stand facing one another.*)

PORTEN
Someone keeps looking over his shoulder while he's walking. Does he have a guilty conscience?

BERGNER
No, he simply looks over his shoulder from time to time.

PORTEN
Someone is sitting there with lowered head. Is he sad?

BERGNER
(*Assumes a modeling pose for her reply.*) No, he simply sits there with lowered head.

PORTEN
Someone is flinching. Conscience-stricken?

BERGNER
(*Answers in another modeling pose.*) No, he's simply flinching.

PORTEN
Two people sit there, don't look at each other, and are silent. Are they angry with one another?

BERGNER
(*Delivers her sentence in a new pose.*) No, they simply sit there, don't look at each other, and are silent!

PORTEN
Someone bangs on the table. To get his way?

BERGNER
(*In a different pose.*) Couldn't he for once simply bang on the table? (*They run toward each other with a little yelp of joy, embrace and separate again at once, looking at one another tensely.* BERGNER *points to* GEORGE.) He's polishing the cutlery and putting it on display on a red cloth. Does he want to sell it? (PORTEN *is standing there with arms hanging down, only shakes her head briefly.* GEORGE, *feeling as if released, now begins to polish the utensils lightheartedly.* BERGNER *points to* JANNINGS, *saying simultaneously*) He turns his back on us, sits in the most comfortable fauteuil. Does that mean he's more powerful than all of us? (PORTEN *looks into her eyes and only shakes her head briefly.* JANNINGS *stretches himself, relieved, in his fauteuil, obviously delighted to have lost his significance.* BERGNER *points with her head to* VON STROHEIM.) He's sitting alone in the corner on a big sofa. Does he want to tell us that we should sit down next to him? (PORTEN *now merely smiles as one does about something that has turned out to be a dream.* VON STROHEIM *also forgets himself, smiles amiably, and is obviously relaxing.*) And the mirror over there?

JANNINGS
(*Gets up and strolls toward the women.*) It's quite a simple mirror.

GEORGE
(*Joins in.*) Perhaps there's a flyspeck on it!

BERGNER
And why can't the drawer be pulled out of the chest?

JANNINGS
(*Hesitates just slightly.*) It's stuck.

BERGNER
And why is it stuck?

VON STROHEIM
(*Jumps off the sofa.*) Let it be stuck!

GEORGE
Yes, let it be stuck!

GEORGE and VON STROHEIM
(*Skip and dance toward each other, lifting their legs like dancing bears.*) Let it be stuck!

JANNINGS
(*Joins them.*) Let it be stuck! Let it be stuck!

GEORGE, VON STROHEIM, JANNINGS
(*The three dance around one another.*) Let it be stuck, the drawer! The drawer, oh, let it be stuck! Let it, the drawer, let it, oh, let it be stuck! (*They sing in unison.*) Oh, let the drawer be stuck, oh, oh, let the drawer be stuck! (*They stand still and sing the same words to the melody of "Whisky, Please Let Me Alone" in a canon with assigned voices, with a break in the middle, after an "Oh," whereupon they all look at one another in silence, raise their index fingers, whereupon one of them continues singing an octave lower: ". . . let the drawer be stuck!" whereupon the other two voices also join in one by one, also an octave lower, and they finish the song in harmony. They all look at one another gravely and tenderly.*) We are free? We are free! (*Pell-mell*) We only

dreamed all that! Did we only dream all that? What? I have already forgotten! And I'm just noticing how I'm forgetting! I'm standing quite still and am myself observing how I gradually forget. I'm trying to remember, but as I'm trying to remember, I notice that it sinks down lower and lower, it is as if I had swallowed something, and with each attempt to regurgitate it, it slips down lower and lower. It is sinking and you loom more and more. Where have you been, I was looking for you?! Who are you? Do I know you? (*They embrace, bend their heads toward one another, hide them, rub them together, caress each other with heads and hands. They separate and busy themselves lightheartedly with the objects: touch them, press them to their bodies, lean playfully against them, prop them up, cradle them in their arms, bring two objects into contact as for an embrace, pinch, pat, and caress them, wipe dust off them, remove hairs from them . . . While doing so, they sigh, hum, giggle, laugh, trill . . . Only once they become briefly uncertain and quiet: one of the women stands leaning against the bannister, her face turned away and her shoulders twitching. After an anxious moment, one of the men walks up to her and turns her timidly around; she is laughing quietly, and by and by they all become merry again.*

At one time one of the men walks from an end of the stage toward the others, who are just walking toward him. He walks as if they will collide, but just when one seems to see them collide he feints with his body and steps elegantly aside. He does that across the entire stage. The other men imitate him, walk toward the women and skirt them elegantly before walking on in the same direction; the three men avoid objects the same way. They are delighted with one another, and the women laugh.

One of them turns a cartwheel; the other leaps merrily over an obstacle over which he could have simply stepped; the third elegantly demonstrates a gesture with his lower arm by lifting the arm and quickly bending the elbow, letting,

*as if by magic, the sleeve slip to the elbow. He repeats this
several times, finally with the same movement giving himself
playfully a light.*

At last, quite as a matter of course, one after the other sits
down by the table, the women in the fauteuils with footstools,
VON STROHEIM *in the fauteuil without footstool,* JANNINGS *in
the easy chair,* GEORGE *in the straight chair. As in an after-
image they still hint at their previous playful acts, still repeat
what they said to one another.*) I forgot myself completely.
"I"? We! We forgot ourselves.

   (*Finally they calm down. Only* BERGNER *is still playing with
her handbag and does not know where to put it.*)

VON STROHEIM
Why don't you leave it on your lap?

JANNINGS
Having something on your lap is most pleasant.

GEORGE
(*It occurred to him simultaneously.*) . . . something on your
lap is most pleasant. (*They laugh.*) In your lap you have the
most pleasant feeling for something.

PORTEN
(*It occurred to her too, but a little later.*) In your lap you
have the most pleasant feeling for something. (*They all
laugh.* BERGNER *cautiously puts the handbag on her lap, and
with little wiggling movements puts herself into a comfortable position in the fauteuil. She emits a small sound.*

   *All of them try what it is like to have things on one's lap,
are satisfied, and put the things back in their places.* PORTEN
shows her naked arm to VON STROHEIM.) You see, I've got
goose pimples.

VON STROHEIM

Are you . . . Do you feel—(*He stops in time.*) So you have
goose pimples, do you? (*He laughs.*)

(*All laugh as if it were an unpleasant memory.*)

PORTEN

Yes, I simply have goose pimples.

(*Pause.* JANNINGS *pulls something out of his upholstered
seat. He holds it up and shows it to* GEORGE. *At the same
time, as if unintentionally, with the index finger of the other
hand he elongates one eye.* GEORGE *ignores that, bends toward what* JANNINGS *has in his hand.*)

VON STROHEIM

(*Also turns his head toward* JANNINGS. *In a playful mood*)
You have something there. What is it? Nothing special, I
assume? Nothing worth mentioning, I hope. There's no
need to talk about it, is there?

(BERGNER *and* PORTEN *turn their heads slightly too, but
look away again immediately.*)

JANNINGS

A pin. (*They all look at it, as though surprised.*)

VON STROHEIM

A pin? You don't mean "the pin"?

JANNINGS

The very one.

PORTEN

And it really exists? It isn't merely a figure of speech?

JANNINGS
Here, see for yourself.

(*He hands the pin to* GEORGE, *who hands it to* VON STRO-
HEIM *very matter-of-factly, who hands it to* PORTEN.)

PORTEN
It has all turned out to be true. Not even the ruby-red pin-
head is missing. It has all come true.

VON STROHEIM
Did you dream about it?

PORTEN
Someone mentioned it in the dream. (*She hands the pin to*
BERGNER.) When I saw the pin just now, I remembered it
again. And I had thought it was also only just another word.

GEORGE
Once someone told me about a corpse with a pinhead-sized
wound on his neck. (*Pause.*) (*To* JANNINGS) Did *you* tell
me about that?

JANNINGS
I can't remember. But when you started telling the story, it
seemed familiar to me, too.

GEORGE
No, it was a movie. (*Pause.*) It was thundering and at the
same time fog banks on the village street . . .

BERGNER
Should I drop it?

(*They all become quiet and do not move. She drops the
pin.*)

GEORGE
(*Negates the effect by speaking again too soon.*) Children
with lumps of plaster on their eyes—(*He breaks off, but it is
already too late. However, they only smile, leave the pin
where it fell.*)

VON STROHEIM
I already told you the story about the lake?

PORTEN
No.

(*He looks at* BERGNER: *she shakes her head tenderly.*)

JANNINGS
(*Simultaneously*) No.

VON STROHEIM
Then I probably only thought of it.

PORTEN
Does it have anything to do with the pin?

VON STROHEIM
I was sitting by a lakeshore in the morning and the lake was
sparkling. Suddenly I noticed: the lake is *sparkling*. It is really
sparkling.

(*Pause.*)

PORTEN
Something similar happened to me one time when someone
told me that his pockets were empty. "My pockets are
empty!" I didn't believe him and he turned his pockets inside
out. They really were empty. Incredible!

(GEORGE *takes a cigar out of the cigar box, then offers the box to* JANNINGS, *who takes out a cigar.* GEORGE *strikes a match and hands it to* JANNINGS; *he lights his cigar and blows out the match.* GEORGE *lights himself another match.*

VON STROHEIM *takes the red cloth from the table, jumps up with it, walks around with it, shakes it as if he wants to demonstrate it to them. They bend forward, inspect.* VON STROHEIM *looks around triumphantly. They nod, shake their heads surprised, laugh with delight, slap their thighs with laughter. Exclamations such as* "A red cloth, indeed!" "No doubt about it!" "Lupus in fabula," "Talk of the devil!" "Atlantis has reappeared!"

VON STROHEIM *stands in front of the others like a magician. He turns all his pockets inside out very fast—the pockets are very wide and light-colored—and strikes a pose.* PORTEN *applauds vigorously.* VON STROHEIM, *as magician, takes off his smoking jacket in a jiffy, turns it over, and already has put it back on.*)

JANNINGS
(*Enthusiastically*) So it is true! (VON STROHEIM *produces a small imitation of a rolling pin out of his pocket, which is now the magician's pocket.* JANNINGS *exclaiming so that the cigar drops out of his mouth*) Not only in jokes then! (GEORGE *hands him the cigar.* JANNINGS *wipes the ash off his knees, stops suddenly, notices what he is doing, continues cleaning in a merry ritual.*) Ash on my suit! When I tell about that, no one will believe me. (*They all laugh.* VON STROHEIM *conjures up the magician's magic cloth, a flag in colors that do not signify a particular country. He blows briskly on the flag, making it flutter.*) Indeed, it flutters! The flag flutters! (VON STROHEIM *stashes the things into his pockets, becomes an actor: he walks to the bar, takes out a bottle, fondles it, then supports himself backward with one hand on the table.* JANNINGS *calmly translates this for* GEORGE.) He is fondling the bottle and supporting himself

with his hand on the table. (VON STROHEIM *moves to the side of the table, dangles the bottle by the neck, and begins to squint.* JANNINGS *to* GEORGE) He is holding the bottle by the neck and squinting. (VON STROHEIM *puts the bottle back and moves through the room with hunched shoulders, making an unnecessarily wide curve around each object but at the same time scrutinizing each.*) He hunches his shoulders, looks at the objects, yet makes a curve around them.

VON STROHEIM
(*Returns to the table. As a teacher*) And now to the practical application: someone fondles an object or leans against it?

GEORGE
The proprietor.

VON STROHEIM
Someone moves with hunched shoulders among objects, makes a curve around them?

GEORGE
The guest.

VON STROHEIM
Someone who is squinting holds an object in his hand?

GEORGE
The thief.

JANNINGS
Someone fondles an object because it belongs to him. Because someone fondles an object, does it belong to him?

VON STROHEIM
Unless you prove the opposite.

JANNINGS
Someone with an object in his hand begins to squint. Because he has stolen it?

VON STROHEIM
Unless he proves his innocence.

JANNINGS
Someone suddenly puckers up his mouth and nose. (*He shows how.*) Because he's afraid and a coward?

VON STROHEIM
Unless his actions prove the opposite.

JANNINGS
But if there's nothing to do?

VON STROHEIM
What else would he be afraid of?

JANNINGS
I don't understand that.

VON STROHEIM
What you're sitting on is an easy chair, isn't it?

JANNINGS
Yes.

VON STROHEIM
Or is it perhaps a life preserver? (JANNINGS *laughs at this extraordinary suggestion.*) It seems just as ridiculous to you when I claim that you are sitting on a life preserver as it would to claim that someone's mouth and nose pucker up (*He imitates it.*) because he feels like doing something.

(*Pause.*)

JANNINGS
But an easy chair is an easy chair, and an expression (*He makes one.*) is an expression. How can the two be compared?

VON STROHEIM
I will demonstrate to you how one can. (*Pause. They all wait. Pause.* VON STROHEIM *suddenly*) What do you have in your mouth? (JANNINGS *quickly takes the cigar out of his mouth and puts it out.* VON STROHEIM *smiles.*) Why is your collar button open? (JANNINGS *nimbly closes his collar button.*) You are so serious?

(JANNINGS *laughs resoundingly. Pause. Quiet. Pause.*)

JANNINGS
(*Softly*) You have something on your nose.

VON STROHEIM
(*Is about to wipe it off, hesitates, softly*) You've understood?

(*Pause.*)

JANNINGS
(*Suddenly loud*) You're just standing there, please hand me the bottle. (VON STROHEIM *plays along, hands him the bottle.*) No, not that one, the other one! (*He points.*) No, not that one, one can't ask for anything any more. Yes, that's the one! (*But he hands the bottle back to him at once.*) Put it back in its place!

VON STROHEIM
(*Like a teacher who is playing a student*) Why?

JANNINGS
Because you took it from its place. (VON STROHEIM *nods, puts the bottle back.*) No, not there. Back in its place, I said. Over there, right.

VON STROHEIM
Why precisely there?

JANNINGS
Because that's where it stood before. (VON STROHEIM *nods.*)
Give me another bottle.

VON STROHEIM
Why?

JANNINGS
Because you gave me a bottle once before.

VON STROHEIM
That's perfect! (*He hands him the bottle.*)

JANNINGS
You're standing? (VON STROHEIM *wants to sit down on a
sofa.*) Back in your place! (VON STROHEIM *sits down in his
place. Playfully* JANNINGS *assigns the following roles: he hits
the bottle neck with a teaspoon:* GEORGE *gets up.* JANNINGS
without looking at him) Cartwheels! (GEORGE *stands there.*)

VON STROHEIM
(*Prompts him.*) Why?

GEORGE
Why?

JANNINGS
Because you did a cartwheel before! (*Pause.* GEORGE *turns a
cartwheel.* JANNINGS *hands him the magazine.* GEORGE *does
not yet understand this language; he doesn't know what to
do with the magazine, glances into it.*) Hand it on.

GEORGE
Why?

JANNINGS

Didn't you also hand on the pin before? (*Pause.* GEORGE *hands the magazine to* VON STROHEIM; *he gives it back to* GEORGE *as if the pages were mixed up.* GEORGE *understands: he arranges the pages and hands the magazine back to* VON STROHEIM, *who puts it on the table.* JANNINGS *pulls the second red cloth from under the cutlery on the table and lets it drop. He points to it with the spoon. Pause.*) Well?

GEORGE
Why?

JANNINGS
Didn't you just do a cartwheel?

GEORGE
But how can you compare the two?

JANNINGS
For whom, then, did you do the cartwheel?

GEORGE
For you—(*He hesitates.*)

JANNINGS
"Of course" you wanted to say, right?

GEORGE
For you, of course.

JANNINGS
If you can do a cartwheel for me, you can also pick up a cloth for me.

(*Pause.*)

GEORGE
(*Wants to bend down for the cloth, hesitates.*) But what
if I don't want to?

JANNINGS
Now it's too late for that. All the time you did as I asked you
to and never said anything. You were content until now or
you would have said something. So why should you be dis-
satisfied now? You didn't contradict me at any time. Why
should you be allowed to contradict me now? No, what you
utter now doesn't count any more. Do as I say! (*Pause.*
GEORGE *picks up the cloth, wants to hand it to* JANNINGS, *who
doesn't even bother to extend his hand, hesitates, lets it drop
again "as if his hand has fallen asleep." Pause.* JANNINGS *in a
sensible tone of voice*) Look at the others. (*He turns his head
to* VON STROHEIM, *then to* PORTEN. VON STROHEIM *goes at
once with the guitar—which he takes out of the bag while
walking—up to* BERGNER, *sits down behind her and quaintly
strikes two soft chords.* PORTEN *sits down on* JANNINGS's
knees and makes herself comfortable.) If they do as they're
told—why don't you too?

(*Pause.*)

GEORGE
But why do they do it?

JANNINGS
First obey. Then we can talk about it. (*Pause.* GEORGE *hands
him the cloth, which* JANNINGS *places picturesquely around*
PORTEN's *shoulders, and ties under her chin. To her*) Well?
(*She kisses him without moving her head.*) Now ask!

GEORGE
Why do they do that? Why do they listen to you?

(VON STROHEIM *strikes another quaint chord.*)

JANNINGS

Because it is natural to them. They did it once without my
saying anything while they were half asleep, or because it
just happened like that. Then I said it and they did it again.
Then they asked me: "May I do that for you?" and I said:
"You shall!" And from then on they did it without my having to say anything. It had become the custom. I could point
my *foot* at something and they would jump and get it.
Nothing but laws of nature. People began to socialize with
one another and it became the rule.

BERGNER

(*On cue, as though talking in her sleep*) How are you; I'm
fine, thanks. (*She sighs.*)

JANNINGS

An order resulted; and for people to continue to socialize
with one another, this order was made explicit: it was
formulated. And once it had been formulated, people had to
stick to it because, after all, they had formulated it. That's
natural, isn't it? Say something! No, don't say anything, *I*
am speaking now. Don't touch that, it's mine! (*He pushes a
candlestick away.*) Don't dare to stare at it, it's my property!
What was I talking about? Help me! No, don't say anything.
About the laws of nature. (*He takes an ashtray into his
hand, then lets it drop.*) Just as this ashtray obeys the law
of gravity, so you obey me. Well? (*He points with his foot;*
GEORGE *puts the ashtray back on the table.*) You see? Do
you believe me now? No, don't answer, I'll answer for you.
Yes, that business with the ashtray and the force of gravity is
true enough, I can imagine your answer to be. Do you know
what the difference is between you and me? (GEORGE *laughs
as though before a joke.*) No, no joke: I *can* imagine you
sometimes, you *must* imagine me always. Why aren't you
laughing? By the way, this reminds me of a real joke: what's
the man's name who invented the chair? Well? Nothing? I'll

help you. What's the man's name who invented the Zeppelin?
(*Pause. He laughs invitingly.*) You're not laughing. O.K.! But
I'll make a note of it. Where was I? Hadn't I asked you to
remind me what else I wanted to talk about? Didn't I see you
nod? Then I only imagined that I saw you nod. Once I
thought of a conversation I had with someone, and I
remembered distinctly how he'd smiled when he answered
me, and then it occurred to me that I had been talking to
him on the telephone! The laws of nature! The trains! The
ocean! He stood where you're standing now! (GEORGE,
startled, steps aside; JANNINGS *bursts out laughing, again
drops the ashtray.*) I'd like to pick it up for you, but I have
to stick to what I said (*To* PORTEN), don't I? (*She nods.*)
I can't say something and then do the opposite of what I've
said. Inconceivable! That would be a topsy-turvy world. Do
you understand that? (PORTEN *tries to reach backward for
the ashtray.*) Stop, that's *his* job! (GEORGE *puts the ashtray
on the table,* VON STROHEIM *touches the guitar almost accidentally: a gentle chord.*) So you understand. Just as the
trains must obey a schedule so that there is no disorder, so
you must obey me. That business with the trains and their
schedule is probably true, you say? I dare you to tell me that!
Keep quiet? Answer! (GEORGE *wants to speak.*) Forget it!
Like a maggot that crawls across one's palm—no, that belongs
somewhere else. The ocean! What are you thinking of just
now? You can't say it? Then you're not thinking of anything. I once lived for some time by the ocean, and since I
lived there, in what categories would you guess I began to
think? In the categories of low and high tide! And that's how
it is generally: (*As though to the audience*) the manner in
which one thinks is determined by the laws of nature! (*Again
to* GEORGE) For example, since I've started taking walks
through the woods, I always think at the sight of the weak
and the strong in terms of the laws of nature. And since I
learned to read menus—(*He pushes* PORTEN *from his knees
and she goes quickly to the sofa, cuddles up on it, and he*

looks toward her.)—I think about women, whether I want
to or not, in the categories of hors d'oeuvre and main dish.
(*She looks at him, but one rather feels the look than actually
sees it.*) She doesn't want it differently—ask her yourself.
She'll show you how. (*He snaps his fingers at her and she
responds.*)

BERGNER

(*As though she had learned a few questions by heart*) Do I
talk too much for you? Are my knees too bony? Am I too
heavy for you? Is my nose too big? Am I too sensible for
you? Do you find me too loud? Are my breasts too small? Do
you think I'm too fat? Am I too fast for you? Am I too
skinny for you? Was I good?

JANNINGS

You see, she herself uses the categories in which one thinks
of her. (*To* PORTEN) Hey! (*She comes back and settles on
his knees.*) When *I* used to be called, to begin with I only
said "yes!" After all, it was possible that they only wanted
to know whether I was still there. Where were we? (GEORGE
puts his hand to the back of his head, lowers the hand again.)
Stop! Repeat that gesture! (GEORGE *repeats it.*) It reminds
me of something. More slowly! (GEORGE *repeats the gesture.*)
The hat! Do you know the song "Me Hat, It Has Three
Corners"? It's a folk song. (*He recites it seriously.*)

> Me hat, it has three corners
> Three corners has me hat
> And if it hadn't three corners
> It wouldn't be me hat.

Ever since I've known that song I am incapable of imagining
a hat with it. A three-cornered hat: an impossible idea! A
hat: an impossible, a forbidden idea! Once I ordered (or
permitted?) a cake to be cut. "Where?" I was asked. Ever
since then I've been unable to imagine a cake. You try draw-

ing a circle in your mind but don't know where to begin.
Finally there's a noise in the brain as if a boiling egg were
popping. Quiet! Shut up! I can imagine what you want to say!
The circle! I become dizzy when I'm supposed to imagine it!
And when I become dizzy, I become furious. For example,
someone asks me what time it is. Can you imagine that there's
someone who has no watch? I certainly can't. Dizziness and
anger! Or: a person looks "desperate," starts all sorts of jobs
but stops them all again at once. Can you imagine anyone
still being seriously desperate? Dizziness! Dizziness and anger!
Or someone is ashamed? Dizziness and anger, dizziness and
anger! Then the contrary: someone is ashamed for someone
else? I for you? At once! You cannot imagine that I'm
ashamed for you? (*He pushes the cigar box off the table so
that all the cigars fall out, puts* PORTEN *in her fauteuil, stands
in front of* GEORGE, *and claps his hands before* GEORGE's *face,
pretending to slap him, and sits down again.*) Like chocolate
and soap—yes, like chocolate that lies next to a piece of
soap. I, at any event, have never felt ashamed—except for
that time when I compared two feelings I had for someone to
chocolate and soap. And then once more. (*Pause.*) And then
the story about the maggot on the palm of the hand. (*Pause.*)
And then once when I was asked: "Who is that?" and answered: "That one? Yes, she's very touching, isn't she?"
(*Pause.*) Yes, and then one more time. (*He laughs shame-
fully, remembering.*) And then once when I said: "Present
company excepted, naturally!" And another time when I
heard someone say, "She's ugly!" and replied: "But she has
pretty eyes." (*Pause.*) And then just the one more time when
I put the matchbook on the counter and the salesman asked
me: "Is that *you?*" (*Pause; puzzled*) Actually, I've been
ashamed quite frequently. (*Pause, to* VON STROHEIM) Should
I make *him* feel ashamed?

VON STROHEIM
(*Strikes the body of the guitar and spreads his fingers.*) Just
so you aren't put to shame by him!

JANNINGS

(*Turns to* GEORGE.) Look over here! (*Successively he takes several objects from the table or out of his pocket and shows them to* GEORGE. GEORGE *looks helplessly at each of them. Finally* JANNINGS *shows him some paper money, waves it, and* GEORGE *quickly tries to grab it.* JANNINGS *laughs.*) This language he understands! This language he understands! (*He laughs again. Pause. They both bow their heads.* JANNINGS *scratches himself once vigorously. Suddenly he points angrily at the cigars.*) What's that?

GEORGE

Cigars.

JANNINGS

And what's that supposed to mean? Pick them up! (GEORGE *bends down.* JANNINGS *giggles.*) Can you still imagine doing anything but what I tell you to? (GEORGE *tries to imagine it. Finally he also starts giggling, but stops again and tries to think once more.*) Imagine you're sitting in my place. (GEORGE *looks up at him. He begins to giggle.* JANNINGS *giggles too, but differently; he looks around himself.* PORTEN *is also giggling.* VON STROHEIM *is smiling.* BERGNER *is absentminded.* GEORGE *collects the cigars and puts them carefully back in the box.* JANNINGS, *while watching him, tells a story.*) Once—(*To* PORTEN) Why are you grinning?

PORTEN

I'm not grinning, I'm smiling.

JANNINGS

Stop fidgeting!

PORTEN

I'm not fidgeting, I'm making myself comfortable.

JANNINGS
Shut your trap!

PORTEN
I don't have a trap.

JANNINGS
(*Has already turned back to his story.*) . . . I had a bad day,
you know how that is. (GEORGE *nods.*) I burned my tongue
on the coffee; as I was tying my shoelaces, I suddenly had
two pieces in my hand, you know what that's like. (GEORGE
nods.) Just as suddenly—why "just as suddenly"? What's the
difference! In any case, as I'm writing down what I plan to
do, the tip of the pencil breaks off. I look for another pencil—
no, not what you're thinking: the pencil does write; however, all at once I noticed that overnight I've begun to write
one letter differently from the way I used to, with a curlicue
where I never before made a curlicue during my entire life!
You know what that's like. (GEORGE *nods, but only after*
JANNINGS *has looked at him.*) To top it all, I suddenly see
before me a woman trampling furiously on eggshells. I tear
her away by the hair, you know what that's like. But it
turns out that she is purposely breaking up the shells for the
birds. Dazed, I walked on and notice another madman. He's
running back and forth on a piece of land, and a crowd has
already formed around him. Then it turns out that he isn't
mad at all but the owner of the land trying to keep people
from trespassing. Even more dazed, I walk on and am
thinking about a goose I'm in the process of carving up, very
fastidiously, you know what I'm like, not to get any grease
stains on my suit, when someone grabs me by the arm from
behind. Despite, or just *because* of, my dazed state—(*He
smirks.*) Whenever I say *despite*, I also must say, *just because
of*—I swiveled around and gave this someone a box on the
ear. My hand slipped; you know what that's like: I thought
someone with greasy fingers had grabbed me. Suddenly—

yes, again *suddenly,* that day passed in leaps and bounds—I stood before a dog that squatted with quivering behind at the curb—*quivering:* I've never used that word before!—and wanted to do his business, you know what that's like. I, no lazybones myself—(*To* GEORGE, *who hesitates*) Don't let me stop you from your work—gave him a kick . . .

PORTEN
Don't go on, please! I don't want to have to dream about it.

GEORGE
Once my mind was on a child and a hot iron, and when I suddenly saw someone reaching for the door handle, I shouted at him: *Don't touch!*

JANNINGS
You can talk and stack cigars *evenly* at one and the same time? (GEORGE *continues to work in silence,* JANNINGS *goes on talking.*) . . . and went home. Luckily the sun set very rapidly, as it always does in the tropics—that's how it is described in all narratives, isn't it?—and as I slowly open the door, there is a soft rustling behind it. (*Slowly* and *softly* generally belong together.) I immediately fired through the panel—and I myself had spread the papers on the floor to frighten the burglars when they'd open the door. A bad day! Later in my rocking chair I dozed off. Suddenly I awake and see the dog running past me. A quick slap with the riding crop—you know what that's like? (GEORGE *nods.*) But it was my own feet: when I jerked awake, I took my black socks for the dog. (*Pause.*) You have nothing to say?

GEORGE
I feel no need to say anything.

JANNINGS
It's enough that I feel the need to hear something from you.

GEORGE
But what if I feel the need to remain silent?

JANNINGS
Then you must say to yourself that in regard to your needs, what matters for you is to learn to need to do what you must do in any case. (*Pause.*) Say something!

(*Pause.*)

GEORGE
But what did you want to prove with the story? You didn't tell the story just to tell a story?

JANNINGS
I told it so you would know what it is like when a whole day passes and one feels out of sorts.

GEORGE
Out of sorts with what?

JANNINGS
With one's work.

GEORGE
You weren't working at the time?

JANNINGS
I was working, but I felt out of sorts with my work.

GEORGE
And what is it like if one feels out of sorts with one's work while one is working?

JANNINGS
I told you: a swift sunset, a rustling behind the door, strange dogs in the room.

GEORGE
And what is it like if one does not feel out of sorts with one's work while one is working?

JANNINGS
It becomes a game.

GEORGE
And how do you manage not to feel out of sorts while you work?

JANNINGS
One must imagine that it's a game.

GEORGE
And who determines the rules of the game?

JANNINGS
The one who plays it: the one who works.

GEORGE
Is it like that or does one have to imagine it?

JANNINGS
If you're not out of sorts, it's like that.

GEORGE
But if I feel out of sorts, then I first have to imagine it?

JANNINGS
If you feel out of sorts, you cannot imagine it. Instead: a swift sunset, a rustling behind the door . . .

GEORGE
But I feel out of sorts.

JANNINGS
I'll show you. (*He gets up and puts a cigar in the box with playful little movements, a finger dance. Then he sits down.*) For me work is a game.

GEORGE
Well, it isn't *your* work. But it is your *thing*. And it's up to you to tell me how *my* work with *your* thing can be called a game. I who feel out of sorts—you're right—cannot imagine it.

(*Pause.*)

JANNINGS
You must regard work like a bet: whoever is faster, more elegant, more thorough—then there are winners and losers.

GEORGE
But with whom am I supposed to bet when I'm by myself?

JANNINGS
With yourself.

GEORGE
Whether I'm faster than myself?

JANNINGS
No smart talk! You can't allow yourself to be ironical until you've finished your work . . . Don't you have two hands?

GEORGE
Obviously.

JANNINGS
Which hand is more nimble?

GEORGE
The right one, I suppose.

JANNINGS

Then make a bet with yourself and give it a try. (*Pause.* GEORGE *starts putting cigars back in the box first with his left, then with his right hand. He becomes increasingly faster, gets into a frenzy. He has finished and puts the box on the table.*) Which hand won?

GEORGE

(*Remains silent. Speaks suddenly.*) Let's bet on something else.

JANNINGS

Fine, let's make a bet.

GEORGE

(*Points to* PORTEN.) You turn her over your knee and spank her.

JANNINGS

And what's the bet?

GEORGE

First turn her over your knee. (JANNINGS *puts* PORTEN *over his knee.*) You hit her with the riding crop as fast as you can for one minute. While doing so you keep your mouth shut. If you open it, you've lost.

JANNINGS

It's a bet. (*Pause. He starts beating her vigorously, but already after a few slaps his lips part. Startled, he lets go of her and sits down, pinches his lips tight. He wipes his forehead.* GEORGE *also sits down. Pause.* VON STROHEIM *touches the guitar as if by chance. A very gentle sound. He laughs.* JANNINGS *opens his mouth as if to roar and wants to hit the table. He shuts his mouth again instantly and lets his fist sink, opens his fingers.*) I believe—(*He breaks off; he wants*

*to reach for something but stops in midair and lets his hand
drop.*)

GEORGE
(*To* PORTEN) You'd better imagine it all once more right
now; then you won't need to dream of it later on—

PORTEN
(*Smiles.*) Of water and of madness, of . . .

VON STROHEIM
(*At the other end, wanted to say something at the same
time.*) I was so very . . .

(*They both break off. Pause.*)

PORTEN
(*Turns again to* GEORGE.) Of water and of madness, of ships
of fools on great rivers where . . .

VON STROHEIM
(*Again at the same time, to* BERGNER) I was so very much
afraid. I was so very much afraid for . . .

(*Pause.*)

JANNINGS
(*Points to* VON STROHEIM *while looking at* PORTEN.) It's his
turn.

(*Pause.*)

VON STROHEIM
(*As in a game, to* BERGNER) I was so very much afraid for
you that I suddenly burst out laughing. You were sitting there
and didn't move. Only your jugular vein throbbed.

BERGNER

I haven't been listening. (*He bends over her, but so that she has to see his face upside down. She opens her eyes, a small cry of horror; he turns his head so that she sees his face normally again, and she calms down instantly and looks at the guitar.*) Is that for me? (VON STROHEIM *hesitates, hands it to her.*) And what do I have to do for that? (*She turns the guitar around as if it were a present, then hands it back.* VON STROHEIM *puts the guitar on the table. He strokes* BERGNER's *neck with his finger. Pause.* BERGNER *slaps his hand.*) Don't touch me!

JANNINGS
(*Prompts.*) Why?

VON STROHEIM
Why don't you want to be touched? You used to let people touch you.

BERGNER
Don't look at me!

VON STROHEIM
A little while ago you looked at me tenderly.

BERGNER
Does that mean that I should "look at you tenderly" now, too? (VON STROHEIM *posts himself in front of her. She looks away.*) Every time you men begin to speak, it is as if a beggar is trying to talk to me.

VON STROHEIM
All of us men?

BERGNER
Yes, you too.

VON STROHEIM
Give me your hand.

BERGNER
Why? (*He takes her hand.*) Are you a palm reader? (VON STROHEIM *strokes her hair.*) I know that my hair is a mess.

VON STROHEIM
You are beautiful.

BERGNER
Have you seen my handbag anywhere?

VON STROHEIM
(*Puts a necklace around her neck.*) What do I get for that?

BERGNER
Why do you have to spoil my necklace for me?

VON STROHEIM
What must I do to make you stop despising me? Is it the way I move that you dislike? Is it my hairline? Is it the way I hold my head that makes you look away? Do the hairs on my hands disgust you? Do you find it exaggerated the way I move my arms up and down when I walk? Do I talk too much? (PORTEN, *watching from some distance away, laughs. Pause.* VON STROHEIM *as on the telephone*) Are you still there? (BERGNER *looks at him.*) Where were you? Why don't you say something? Do say something! Come back! You were so beautiful, it was painful to look at you; so beautiful that I was suddenly very much afraid for you. You were so painfully beautiful that you left me behind—me, who was suddenly so alive—left me behind—terribly *alone.* You said nothing, and I talked to you as one talks to those who have just died: Why don't you say something? Do say something! Can you imagine it?

(*Pause.*)

BERGNER
Not any more. For a moment—(*Pause.*) No. It's over.

VON STROHEIM
Don't stop talking, I am afraid to break in when you stop talking. Right now my tenderness for you is so vehement that I want to hit you.

(*Pause. He hits her. She stands up. He stares at her. She lets him stare at her.*
Abandoning the long rigidity, she moves slowly and walks up and down in front of him. She interrupts her smooth movements now and then to turn jerkily, leans her hand on the hip, stretches herself loosely, lets her arms drop, while moving like this, grazes a number of objects, supports herself everywhere, once swings around to VON STROHEIM, *stops in front of him, takes off her necklace. She is standing there as if she has just come through a door and has leaned against it. She strokes him with the necklace and lets it drop into his pocket.*)

BERGNER
(*Looks at him.*) Don't move! (*He wants to touch her, she stands still, smiling; he hesitates briefly, now touches her neck and wants to pull her toward him; but he is a moment too late, her neck resists him, she shakes off his hand and steps back.*) Why don't you look at me as if you didn't care?

VON STROHEIM
For that I would have to imagine that you were mine.

BERGNER
Then imagine it.

VON STROHEIM
Where should I begin?

BERGNER

(*Points to the guitar.*) Does that belong to you? (*She shoves it away contemptuously.*)

VON STROHEIM

The longer I look at you, the ghostlier you seem to me.

BERGNER

And with every one of your feelings you describe to me you take a possible feeling away from me.

VON STROHEIM

I'm not describing my feelings for you.

BERGNER

But you're *intimating* them. And every time you intimate your love for me, my feelings for you grow duller and I shrivel up. Your feelings move me, but I can't respond to them, that's all. At first I loved you, you were so serious. It struck me that usually it can be said only of a child that it is "serious." Besides (*She laughs.*), you had such beautiful eating habits. You really ate beautifully! And when I once said, "I got wet to the skin!" you said, "To *your* skin!" When I speak of it I almost love you again. (*She embraces him suddenly, but immediately steps back again even farther away.*) But I only have to mention that and I become insensitive right away. You talked all the time and I forgot you more and more. Then I was startled and you were still there . . . A complete stranger, you talked to me with shameless intimacy, as to someone at the end of a movie. Do you understand? I am taboo for you! Suddenly I was taboo for you. Two seconds! Two seconds of pain, that's what having loved you will mean to me later on. (*Pause.*) I'm not disappointed, I'm not sad, I'm only tired of you. (*She moves imperceptibly under her dress.*) I have wronged you so much.

VON STROHEIM
Wronged in what way?

BERGNER
The wrong of loving you.

(PORTEN *suddenly claps her hands vehemently,* GEORGE *laughs offensively,* VON STROHEIM *and* BERGNER *slowly move away from the spot and begin to walk around aimlessly in different directions. Pause.*)

JANNINGS
(*Begins telling a story.*) A short time ago I saw a stewardess, but an ugly one . . .

VON STROHEIM
(*Interrupts him.*) Let's talk about something else.

JANNINGS
(*Begins another story.*) Not long ago I saw a woman standing in the street, not a streetwalker, I must add . . .

GEORGE
(*Interrupts him.*) Something else!

JANNINGS
It is less than a week ago that I saw behind a bank counter someone who had a rather long nose. But when I talked to him, it turned out that despite . . .

PORTEN and BERGNER
(*Interrupt him.*) Let's change the subject.

JANNINGS
All right. No more than five minutes had passed when a man in the park approached me. No, not a faggot . . .

(*He is interrupted by a girl who comes onstage from the right, a suitcase in her hand:* ALICE KESSLER. *She is wearing an afternoon dress and looks as if she had come to this performance by mistake.*)

ALICE
(*Puts down the suitcase, begins to speak very matter-of-factly.*) Is it you? Am I in the right place here? I heard you talking from a distance and came in. The sounds I heard were so inviting, voices and laughter, what is more beautiful than that? What are you showing to each other there, I'd like to see something too. What are you whispering about? I'd like to hear something too. (*She tosses her hat to* VON STROHEIM. *He is so disconcerted that he turns aside instead of catching it.*) How are you? (*Pause. All of them seem petrified.*) How are you?

BERGNER
(*Suddenly loosens up and moves. She practices her reply.*) Fine? Fine. Fine! We're fine. Indeed! We're fine! (*Pause. She tries to talk normally again.*) And how—and how are you?

ALICE
(*Answers quite naturally.*) I'm fine too. Though my hand is still trembling from carrying that heavy suitcase, and I'm still a little weak in the knees because I'm not used to wearing high-heeled shoes; but I can put up with all that because I'm so happy to see you. What are you doing here?

BERGNER
(*Is glad to be able to answer so simply.*) We're talking.

ALICE
And now you don't know how to go on?

BERGNER
Perhaps. (*She falters.*) Yes. Yes!

ALICE
Hello!

BERGNER
Hello!

ALICE
(*To the others*) Hello! (*They raise their heads, perplexed. As if awakening, still half asleep, not knowing yet what they are saying, they say one after the other: "Hello!" Then they comprehend what they have said and become lively. The stage light gradually turns into early-morning light again.*) What time is it?

(GEORGE *nudges* JANNINGS *in the hip.*)

JANNINGS
(*As if back to sleep already*) Don't you have a watch? (*He gives a start.*) "How late is it?" Of course: how late is it? Well, how late is it now? You could have said so right away. (*He opens his pocket watch in front of* ALICE.)

ALICE
Thanks! (*He shuts the watch again.*)

JANNINGS
(*After a pause.*) Don't mention it. (*He spreads his arms wide as if he just found a solution and plays with the answer.*) Don't mention it! (*To* GEORGE) Ask me what time it is.

GEORGE
(*Merrily*) What time is it? (JANNINGS *shows him the pocket watch.*) Thanks!

JANNINGS
(*Shuts the watch.*) Don't mention it.

GEORGE
(*Merrily*) Thanks!

JANNINGS
(*Cheerfully*) But I insist: don't mention it!

(ALICE *holds out her hand to* JANNINGS. *He shakes it instantly. She also holds out her hand to* GEORGE *and he shakes it instantly. She holds out her hand to* PORTEN *and* PORTEN *shakes it gratefully.* VON STROHEIM *understands too and takes her hand.*

Now she takes off her gloves and everyone watches very inquisitively. She hands them to VON STROHEIM *and he takes them. He now picks up the hat and tosses it playfully to* GEORGE. GEORGE *catches the hat and puts it on the table.* VON STROHEIM *adds the gloves to it. Everything is working well.* BERGNER *sits down, apparently relieved.*)

ALICE
(*To* VON STROHEIM) What do you have there in your hand?

VON STROHEIM
(*Opens his fist.*) A necklace. Yes, a necklace!

ALICE
It's beautiful!

A VOICE
(*From the wings*) It's *not* beautiful.

(ELLEN KESSLER *now appears from the left, also with a suitcase, dressed exactly like* ALICE. *She tosses* VON STROHEIM *her hat, then takes off her gloves and hands them to him.*)

VON STROHEIM
(*Puts the things on the table and asks* ELLEN) So you would
like to have it?

ALICE
(*Replies*) Yes.

(*He turns to* ALICE *and puts the necklace around her neck.
She moves voluptuously.*

ELLEN *begins to walk around. She walks about with the
same movements as* ALICE *did before. Shakes hands with
everyone and says: "Hello!" They answer her—at least, the
first two do—after an initial pause; then they laugh at each
other as over a joke. Behind her back* GEORGE *takes a cigar
out of the box and shows it to* JANNINGS; *then he takes out a
second one; they laugh silently; finally* GEORGE *shows* JAN-
NINGS *a third cigar,* JANNINGS *becomes serious and looks to
the left and right, but no one else appears.*

In the meantime, ELLEN *taps* VON STROHEIM *on the shoulder
to greet him. He is talking to* ALICE.)

VON STROHEIM
Why is it that I'm so sure I've seen you before whenever I
look at you, although when I actually say it (*He turns to*
ELLEN, *since she has tapped him on the shoulder, and continues talking to her as if it were quite normal.*), it strikes
me as the usual cliché? (ELLEN *holds out her hand to him
and he bends over it. She shies back, and* ALICE *says, "He
bit me!" remaining motionless, while* ELLEN *performs the
appropriate gestures.* VON STROHEIM *to* ALICE) In my imagination I was about to pinch myself in the arm.

ALICE
(*Motionless.*) Already forgotten.

VON STROHEIM
Already forgotten?

ALICE
You always ask. Were you alone too long?

VON STROHEIM
Why?

ELLEN
Or did you work too hard?

VON STROHEIM
Why?

ALICE
Or do you pose counterquestions only to win time for your reply? Because you're figuring out a lie? Because in the meantime you're so washed up that you can't answer any more without lying? I came in quietly and you all sat there looking washed up, but you looked at me as though *you* had been quiet until then, and *I*, by entering so suddenly, should actually be the one to look washed up.

VON STROHEIM
What are you talking about?

ELLEN
About you. I only wanted to show you how you talk.

(*She leans against his back, shoves one leg between his. He looks down at himself. She puts her arms around his neck.* ALICE *waves to him with a finger.* ELLEN *doubles the gesture by holding her hands to his face from the back and also bending a finger. He wants to take a step forward, and lean back at the same time, but remains standing there.*)

VON STROHEIM
I'll talk as I please.

(ELLEN *puts her hand over his eyes.*)

ALICE
Then say something.

VON STROHEIM
(*Opens his mouth and shuts it. He moves his hands as if he were looking for something that keeps eluding him. He stammers, but whenever his hand seems to seize something, he produces whole syllables: "be, what, un, re"; then he reaches for it and it escapes him again, and he goes on stammering.* ELLEN *takes her hands away from his eyes and he calms down instantly.*) I can't; it's like reaching for a piece of soap under water.

ALICE
What?

VON STROHEIM
Already forgotten. When you covered my eyes, I had it perfectly clear in front of me, but now I have forgotten it. (*He falters.*) "Already forgotten!" That was it! You said, "Already forgotten!" and I remembered something, but what? It escaped me again and again, and I had a feeling like searching for a piece of soap under water—(*He makes a perfunctory gesture, suddenly sniffs his fingers, repeats the gesture. Pause.*)

ELLEN
Perhaps you'll think of it . . .

ALICE
. . . if you watch me?

ELLEN

(*With a flattering voice, ambiguously.*) Perhaps, if you watch me, you'll also remember where you put me—(*She laughs.*) where you carried me to—(*She laughs.*) in those days, do you remember?—(*She laughs.*) and you'll also remember what you should do with me now. (*She laughs. Because* ELLEN *stands behind him, one does not see her talking, although* ALICE *moves her lips and makes the appropriate gestures.*)

(*They let him stand there and skip and dance across the stage side by side. With a fervent pleasure in their work, nearly parallel in their movements, they busy themselves with the objects and with the people: while one takes off* JANNINGS's *boots, the other is loosening* GEORGE's *shoelaces: finished at the same time, they begin to brush* PORTEN's *and* BERGNER's *hair; again they finish at the same time and skip over to the open drawer of the chest; they return with four fancy cushions and stuff them, running helter-skelter but with similar movements, behind the backs of the four people. There is hardly time to perceive these actions when they are already back at the table with four glasses and two bottles and they place them before the characters.*

But now their movements slow down and begin to contradict each other; the work of the one is revoked by the other: one takes the glasses and bottles which the other has placed there away again; one dishevels the hair the other has just brushed; then one takes away the cushions from the persons to whom the other has given them. At the same time the other removes the bottles and the glasses that the one . . . Then one ties the shoelaces the other has untied, while the other in the meantime is taking away the cushions from . . . whereupon the one dishevels the hair that . . . while the other puts JANNINGS's *boots back on.*

However, they stop at the same time and want to run offstage quickly in opposite directions; they return once more

*and change directions, finally run into the wings. As soon as
they have disappeared, they cannot be heard running any
more.*

*Everyone onstage is holding his breath. Suddenly, out of
their state of complete immobilization,* JANNINGS *and* GEORGE
*leap up and rush to the suitcases that have been left onstage.
They fling them into the wings after* ELLEN *and* ALICE, *but no
crashing sound can be heard. They listen. Then they stop
listening. While they are returning to their places,* PORTEN
*suddenly leaps up too and throws the remaining things, hats
and gloves, into the wings after the girls, tossing the hats as
if they were gloves, letting the gloves sail through the air as
if they were hats. One hears them crashing like suitcases.*

They all settle in their places.)

PORTEN
Goo—(*as in good*)

(*The others turn instantly to* BERGNER.)

PORTEN
I'm speaking. (*They turn awkwardly to her.* BERGNER *seems
to have fallen asleep.*) Hello!

GEORGE
(*A little too late.*) Hello!

PORTEN
(*A little too late.*) How are you?

GEORGE
(*A little too late.*) Fine. (*A little too late.*) And how are you?

PORTEN
(*A little too late.*) Fine— Please hand me the paper.

(*A brief pause. Only then does* GEORGE *hand her the newspaper from the table. She holds it in her hand. Pause. Only then does she look into it.*)

GEORGE
Is there anything in it?

(*Pause.*)

PORTEN
(*As though she had answered immediately*) I'm just looking. (*Pause. She puts the paper away.*)

GEORGE
Give me the paper. (*Pause. Then she gives him the paper, but does so as if she had given it to him at once.* GEORGE *opens it, looks at it only after an interval. Pause. Then he exclaims as if he had seen the picture on first glance.*) Ice floes!

(*Pause.*)

PORTEN
(*Lively*) Really? (*Pause.*) How much do you weigh?

(*Pause.*)

GEORGE
Two hundred eighteen pounds.

(*Pause.*)

PORTEN
O God!

(*Pause.*)

JANNINGS
(*Shakes his head. He hesitates and looks at* GEORGE.) Why are
you shaking your head? Do you want to contradict me?

GEORGE
I am neither shaking my head nor would I, even if I shook
my head, thereby want to contradict you.

PORTEN
(*To* JANNINGS) You were shaking your head yourself.

JANNINGS
That was me?

VON STROHEIM
That was you.

JANNINGS
(*Looks to* GEORGE.) Who is speaking?

VON STROHEIM
I am.

JANNINGS
(*To* VON STROHEIM) That was you?

GEORGE
Yes.

JANNINGS
(*To* GEORGE) You're *talking*?

GEORGE
Are you dreaming?

JANNINGS

>Am I in earth, in heaven, or in hell?
>Sleeping or waking, mad or well-advised?
>Known unto these, and to myself disguised:
>Am I transformed, master, am not I?

(*Pause. To* GEORGE) Do you have a match?

GEORGE

Yes.

(*Pause.* JANNINGS *points with his finger on the table, but the others look at his finger. At last he looks at his finger too and lets his hand drop. Pause.* VON STROHEIM *wants to pull out the red cloth.*)

JANNINGS

(*Sees it and screams*) No! (VON STROHEIM *puts it away again instantly. Pause.* PORTEN *begins to laugh, becomes quiet immediately.* GEORGE *looks at her questioningly, she only shakes her head. Pause.*) Let us pray to God.

PORTEN

(*Instantly*) My candy.

BERGNER

(*In her sleep*) There's a rat in the kitchen.

(*Pause.*)

VON STROHEIM

(*Reaches into the cigar box. He asks*) May I take one? (*They look at him, he pulls back his hand. He asks once more*) May I take a cigar? (*And already extends his hand. They look at him and he pulls back his hand. With arms pressed to his sides, he asks once more*) May I take one?

(*No one looks at him and he takes a cigar.* PORTEN *gives him the ashtray.*)

GEORGE
(*To* PORTEN) Thank you.

PORTEN
Why are you thanking me?

GEORGE
Because that would have been my job.

   (*Long pause.* GEORGE *lifts up the teapot and puts it down again.*)

JANNINGS
(*Upbraids him.*) What do you mean by that?

GEORGE
(*Pulls in his head. Pause. He takes out a piece of chocolate candy, removes the silver foil, and eats the candy. After he has consumed it, he asks* PORTEN) Or did you want a piece of it? (*She doesn't reply. He stares into the paper.*) Just now I read the word *snowstorm,* and now I can't find it any more!

   (*All stare into the paper. Pause.*)

VON STROHEIM
(*To* PORTEN) Do you have the number 23–32–322?

PORTEN
No, I have the number 233–23–22. (*Brief pause.*) In my neighborhood there is a shopping center with stores, restaurants, and . . .

VON STROHEIM
A movie house?

PORTEN

Why? (*Pause.*) I once attended a going-out-of-business
sale . . .

GEORGE

And everyone screamed, ran around, and turned over the
furniture?

PORTEN

No. They— Yes! They turned over the furniture, screamed,
and ran around! (*She looks at him happily, becomes serious
again instantly. Suddenly delighted, to* VON STROHEIM) 23–
32–322? Yes, that *is* my number. (*Pause. She looks at* GEORGE
for a long time.)

GEORGE

Why do you look at me like that?

PORTEN

I'm afraid I might not be able to recognize you again. (*She
was serious when she began her reply but ended it as a joke.
She cuddles her head against her shoulder. Pause.* GEORGE
lowers his head.) Hey!

GEORGE

(*Shouts at her.*) What kind of a feeling do you have? (*He
comes to his senses and asks her again kindly*) I wanted to
ask you: what kind of feelings do you have?

PORTEN

Too many of them.

JANNINGS

In those days the grass smelled of dog piss before the thunderstorm.

PORTEN
Who's saying that?

JANNINGS
I?

PORTEN
I see. (*She continues at once.*) As a child, if I wanted to have something, I always had to say first what it was called.

GEORGE
(*Wants to say something.*) And I . . .

VON STROHEIM
(*Irritated*) Yes, people showed me something and then walked away with it—(*Contemplatively*) And I had to follow and get it for myself.

GEORGE
(*Wants to say something.*) And I . . .

VON STROHEIM
Or people simply opened the drawer in which the thing was and went away.

GEORGE
(*To* VON STROHEIM) And so that I could learn to get my way—(VON STROHEIM *looks away.* GEORGE *turns to* JANNINGS.) I was shoved toward the objects that someone had taken from me. (JANNINGS *looks away and* GEORGE *turns to* PORTEN.) I was supposed to get them back myself.

PORTEN
(*Remembering*) Yes! How I fidgeted then!

VON STROHEIM
(*While looking away, speaks to* JANNINGS, *who is clearing his throat.*) You were about to say something?

JANNINGS
No.

(*Pause.*)

GEORGE
How strange! (*With this exclamation he wants to call attention to himself, but no one turns to him. Instead,* PORTEN *winks at* JANNINGS, *who thereupon puts a finger to his lips and shakes his head.* VON STROHEIM *then bends forward and elongates an eye with one finger. This time attention is paid to the sign: as a reply* JANNINGS *pulls his mouth apart with two fingers; thereupon* VON STROHEIM *turns up the lapel of his jacket by grasping it conspicuously with thumb and little finger, and* JANNINGS *nods twice.* PORTEN, VON STROHEIM, *and* JANNINGS *laugh.*) Strange!

PORTEN
(*Asks him almost reluctantly*) What's strange?

GEORGE
(*Relieved*) Suddenly I remembered a hill I had climbed with someone and the cloud shadows that appeared and vanished.

PORTEN
And what's strange about that?

GEORGE
That I should remember it so spontaneously.

PORTEN

(*Cleans her eye as if he had spit at her during his discourse. Very hostile*) Put your paper there away.

GEORGE

It's not my paper.

PORTEN

(*Snaps the paper away.*) And move your cup away from there. (*She snaps her fingers against the cup so that it turns over.*)

GEORGE

It isn't my cup.

PORTEN

And spare me your recollections. (*She instantly continues kindly to* VON STROHEIM) Do you know the expression "To mention the noose in the house of the man who's been hanged"?

(JANNINGS *laughs,* VON STROHEIM *smiles.*)

GEORGE

Why are you so hostile?

PORTEN

And why are you so pale?

GEORGE

I'm not pale!

PORTEN

And I'm not hostile! (*She continues at once.*) Do you know the expression "To place one's hands on one's head"?

GEORGE
(*Looks at* JANNINGS; *then replies.*) Certainly.

PORTEN
Why do you look at *him* before answering?

GEORGE
It's a habit.

PORTEN
Put your hands on your head. (*He hesitates.*) Did you hear what I said?

GEORGE
(*Again first looks at* JANNINGS.) I'm still thinking about it.

PORTEN
But the expression exists, doesn't it?

(GEORGE *slowly places his hands on his head.*)

VON STROHEIM
(*Is playing along.*) Put your hands on the table.

GEORGE
(*Tests whether the sentence exists.*) "Put your hands on the table." (*Relieved*) Yes. (*He puts his hands on the table.*)

PORTEN
Make your hands into fists and caress me!

GEORGE
(*Tests the sentence.*) "Make your hands into fists and caress me!?" No!

VON STROHEIM
Hand me the cup.

(GEORGE *hands him the cup unthinkingly.*)

PORTEN
I'll show you something (*She smiles at* VON STROHEIM *as her initiate and starts searching in her clothes. Eventually* GEORGE *stretches out his hand while she is still looking. Now and then she looks at his hand and continues to search. Suddenly she hits his hand and shoves it away. Maliciously*) That's what I wanted to show you.

(*He writhes and draws in his head. All at once she covers her eyes with both hands and shudders.*)

GEORGE
(*Startled*) What's the matter?

PORTEN
(*Takes her hands from her eyes.*) Oh, it's nothing. (GEORGE *wants to reach for the cup that* VON STROHEIM *has put down in the meantime, but* VON STROHEIM *displaces it a little and* GEORGE *withdraws his hand. They repeat this maneuver several times, both displaying a lot of patience.* PORTEN *interrupts the game; very hostile to* GEORGE) Who are you? (GEORGE *gets up quickly and assumes a pose behind the table as if his picture were about to be taken.*) Now I remember. You're the salesman. You gave me the . . . (*She puts the riding crop on the table. She makes a slip of the tongue.*) How much is it?

GEORGE
Riding crop.

PORTEN
Yes, that's want I wanted to ask too. You sold me the riding crop.

(GEORGE *sits down,* PORTEN *again puts her hands over her eyes and shudders. She pushes the riding crop away.*)

JANNINGS
Don't you like it any more?

PORTEN
No, I only pushed it away.

JANNINGS
(*In a disguised voice*) The *riding crop* on the table, that means: someone who's very close to you will be swallowed up by a swamp and you will stand there slowly clapping your hands above your head. (*He laughs in a strange voice.* PORTEN *gets up quickly, pushing the guitar off the table in the process.* JANNINGS *in a disguised voice*) A *guitar* falls off the table, that means: hats staggering into glacial fissures during the next mountain-climbing expedition. (*He laughs in a strange voice.*)

VON STROHEIM
(*To* PORTEN, *who is standing motionless*) You want to leave?

PORTEN
(*Sits down.*) No, I stood up just now. (*She suddenly crosses her arms over her breast and hunches her shoulders.*)

GEORGE
Are you cold?

PORTEN
(*Drops her arms.*) No. (*To* VON STROHEIM) And who are you? (VON STROHEIM *picks up the guitar and holds it as he*

did previously. PORTEN *tenderly*) Oh, it's you! (*She becomes serious again immediately.*)

VON STROHEIM
Did you remember something?

(*Helplessly, she tries to give him another affectionate look, stops, reaches for a cigar.*)

GEORGE
Are you restless?

PORTEN
(*Puts the cigar back in the box. Serene*) No, I only wanted to take a cigar. (*Suddenly she screams*) I only wanted to take a cigar! (GEORGE *shies back, pulls his jacket over the head, as if he were protecting himself against rain, and stays hunched up like that.* PORTEN *screams*) I only wanted to take a cigar! I ONLY WANTED TO TAKE A CIGAR!

(*They all hunch up more and more. Now one hears a noise emanating from backstage, a high-pitched, pathetic howling.*
The howling coincides with a slight darkening onstage. PORTEN *immediately stops and hunches up too.*
The WOMAN WITH THE SCARF *steps swiftly out of the wings and walks to the second tapestry door without looking at anyone. As soon as she opens the door, there is quiet behind it. Instead, one hears the rustling of a newspaper, which is lying just inside the door. The* WOMAN *goes inside and returns with a big* DOLL *that represents a* CHILD. *The* CHILD *is quiet now, it has the hiccups. It is wearing a gold-embroidered white nightgown and looks very true to life. The mouth is enormous and open. As the* WOMAN *reaches center stage with the* CHILD, *it starts to bawl terribly, somehow without any preliminaries.* GEORGE, *jacket over his head, quickly leaps toward the chest and closes the drawer. The bawling stops at once.*

The WOMAN *carries the* CHILD *now from one to the other very fast, and in passing, during brief stops, it reaches for the women's breasts and between the men's legs. Very rapidly it also wipes off all the things that had been lying on the table, then pulls away the lace tablecloth and drops it. When the* WOMAN *stands with the* CHILD *beside* BERGNER, *who seems to be still asleep, it begins to bawl again, and as suddenly as if it had never stopped. The* WOMAN *holds it in such a way that the* CHILD *sees* BERGNER *from the front. It stops bawling at once and is carried away.*

The WOMAN *returns alone, closes the tapestry door, and goes off. After she has gone, they all sit there motionless. One of them tries to reach for something, but stops as soon as he starts. Someone else tries a gesture that atrophies instantly. A third wants to reply with a gesture, interrupts it twitching. They squat there, start to do something simultaneously; one of them futilely tries to pull his hand out of a pocket; one or two of them even open their mouths—a few sounds, then all of them grow stiff again and cuddle up, make themselves very small as if freezing to death.*

Only BERGNER *sits there the whole time motionless, with eyes closed. All of a sudden, as though she were playing "waking up," she moves slightly. By and by, the others look toward her.* VON STROHEIM *gets up and bends down to her. She again moves a little. The others are motionless. She opens her eyes and recognizes* VON STROHEIM; *she begins to smile.)*

The stage becomes dark.

Translated by Michael Roloff

They Are Dying Out

*"It suddenly occurs to me that I am
playing something that doesn't even
exist, and that is the difference. That is
the despair of it."*

Characters

HERMANN QUITT
HANS, *his confidant*
FRANZ KILB, *minority stockholder*
HARALD VON WULLNOW ⎤
BERTHOLD KOERBER-KENT ⎟ *businessmen and friends*
KARL-HEINZ LUTZ   ⎬   *of* QUITT
PAULA TAX   ⎟
QUITT'S WIFE   ⎦

Act I

A *large room. The afternoon sun is shining in from one side. The distant silhouette of a city, as though it were seen through a huge window, is visible in the background. (The background might also be formed by a backdrop, similar to a movie screen, with the silhouette of the city vaguely outlined against it.)*
QUITT, *wearing a sweat suit, is working out on a punching bag, belaboring it with his fists, feet, and knees.* HANS, *his confidant, wearing tails, stands next to him with a tray and a bottle of mineral water, watching.* QUITT *takes a sip from the bottle, pours some on his head, and sits down on a stool.*

QUITT
I feel sad today.

HANS
So?

QUITT
I saw my wife in a dressing gown and her lacquered toes and suddenly I felt lonely. It was such a no-nonsense loneliness

that I have no trouble speaking about it now. It relieved me, I crumbled, melted away in it. The loneliness was objective, a quality of the world, not something of myself. Everything stood with its back to me, in gentle harmony with itself. While I was taking a shit I heard the sounds I was making as if they came from a stranger in the next cubicle. When I took the bus to the office—

HANS
So as to maintain contact with the people and to study their needs. For the purpose of R and D?

QUITT
—the sad curve which the bus described at one point at a wide traffic circle cut like a yearning dream deep into my heart.

HANS
The world's sorrow
Cut Mr. Quitt's feelings
To the marrow.
Hold on to your senses, Mr. Quitt. Someone as wealthy as you can't afford these moods. A businessman who talks like that, even if he really feels like that, is only giving a campaign speech. Your feelings are a luxury and are useless. They might be useful to those who could live according to them. Mr. Quitt: for example, why don't you make *me* a gift of the sorrows from your leisure time to reflect about my work. Or—

QUITT
Or?

HANS
Or become an artist. You're already supporting violin recitals; you even condescended to collect money in public for the

acquisition of a painting by the National Gallery. The wealth of feelings that is yours as of any given date this month is not only useful but is even essential for an artist. Why don't you paint the curve, the curve of yearning which your bus described, on canvas? Why don't you sell your experience as a painting?

QUITT

(*Stands up.*) Hans, you're playing your daily role as if you knew it by rote. More realistically, please! More lovingly! Grander!

HANS

And the way Mr. Quitt just stepped out of his role—was that pure make-believe too?

QUITT

Let's not start splitting hairs. I admit: the salesgirl in the aforementioned bus eating French fries that smelled of rancid oil ruined my feelings—well, I would have loved to have slapped her face. On the other hand: shortly afterwards I met a black on the street; he was completely absorbed in the photos he'd just picked up from the drugstore, grinning to himself, swept away in remembrance, so that I suddenly remembered along with him, I felt solidarity with him. You're laughing. But there are moments when one's consciousness, too, takes a great leap forward.

HANS

But brutal reality
In no time destroys
That sense of solidarity.
However, I am laughing because you told me many times how you like to remember the time when you lived for days on end in Paris on nothing but French fries and ketchup.

QUITT

I had guests when I was telling that story. And in company, I sometimes also mention "the wood anemones and the hazelnut bushes from the springtime of my youth."

HANS

Does the addition of these artistic elements facilitate negotiations?

QUITT

Yes: by serving as an allegory for what is being left unsaid. The wood anemones beneath the hazelnut bushes then signify something altogether different. Only those who speak know that. The poetic element is for us a manifestation of the historic element, even if it is only a convention. Without poetry we would be ashamed of our deals, would feel like primordial man. By the way, just who exactly is coming today?

HANS

Harald von Wullnow
Karl-Heinz Lutz
Berthold Koerber-Kent
Paula Tax
all of them businessmen and friends of Quitt.

QUITT

I still have to change. If my wife comes, tell her to take care of the guests—then we can be sure that she'll go "bargain hunting" instead of flushing the toilet the whole time. Incidentally, I feel genuinely sad. Almost a comfortable feeling. (*Exit.*)

HANS

How easily Mr. Quitt talks about himself! You have to envy him his sadness. He becomes talkative then, like someone who's being filmed. In any event, time passes more quickly with a sad Quitt, because when he feels good he is distant, unapproachable, rubs his hands together briskly, hops up and down once, that's his Rumpelstiltskin act. (*He sits down on the stool.*) And what about me? What was I allowed to feel this morning? Isn't it true that you can tell more stories about yourself when you've just woken up than at any other time? Thus: the sun rose and shone into my open mouth. I hadn't had any dreams. I even find it repulsive the way people purse their mouth when they say "dream." When I brushed my teeth my gums bled. I would have liked to do it. But there was nothing doing. I: made a list of the meat to be ordered. Who am I, where did I come from, where am I going? Me . . . Yes, me, me! Always me. Why not some-one else? (*He reflects and shakes his head.*) I have to try it when I'm with people. (*He gets up.* MINORITY STOCKHOLDER KILB *appears in the background.*) I can't remember anything personal about myself. The last time anyone talked about me was when I had to learn the catechism. "Your humble ser-vant" of "Your Grace." Once I had a thought but I forgot it at once. I'm trying to remember it even now. So I never learned to think. But I have no personal needs. Still, I can indulge in a few gestures. (*He raises his fist but pulls it down again at once with the other hand. Now he notices* KILB.) Who are you, where did you come from, and so forth?

KILB
My name is Franz Kilb. (HANS *laughs.*) Don't you like the name?

HANS
It's something else. I was talking to myself just now—fluently almost. We don't have anything against names here. And *what* are you?

KILB
A minority stockholder.

HANS

The minority stockholder, perhaps?

KILB

Yes, *the* minority stockholder, Franz Kilb, the terror of the boards of directors, the clown of the stockholders' meetings, the tick in the navel of the economy with the nuisance value of 100—it's me, perking up again. (HANS *steps forward and puts one fist in front of* KILB's *face while showing him out with the other hand.*) Are you serious?

HANS

(*Steps back and drops his arms.*) I'd like to be. But I'm only serious when Mr. Quitt is serious. Nonetheless: it is my honor—scram! (KILB *sits down on the stool.*) So now you're going to tell us the story of your life, is that it?

KILB

I own one share of every major corporation in the country. I travel from one stockholders' meeting to the next and spend the nights in my sleeping bag. I go by bike—see, look at the trouser clips. I'm a bachelor in the prime of life, my reflexes function perfectly. (*He strikes his kneecap and his foot hits* HANS.) This is my Boy Scout knife; during the Second World War I passed my lifeguard test, I can pull you out of the water with my teeth. There are people who hold me in high esteem, but I don't put my name on any political endorsements. I once appeared on *What's My Line?*, I said I was self-employed, no one guessed what I did. At stockholders' meetings I sit with my rucksack and keep my hand up all the time. Stockholders' meetings where the board ignores someone who asks for the floor are null and void. How quiet it is here. Can you hear how quietly I am speaking? My last mistress called me demonic, the press (*He quickly proffers a few newspaper clippings.*) calls me a gadfly. I am quicker than you think. (*He has tripped up* HANS, *who has fallen on his knees.*) I live from my dividends and am a free person, in every respect. My motto is: "Anyone who's for me gets nothing from me; anyone against me will get to know me." That's a warning for you.

(QUITT *returns.* KILB *gets up at once, makes a bow, and steps into the background.*)

QUITT
The ubiquitous Mr. Kilb. (*To* HANS) Stop dusting your tails. As I was looking in the mirror while changing, it struck me as ridiculous that I was growing hair. These insensitive, indifferent threads. I was sitting on the bed, my head in my hands. After some time, I thought: If I keep holding my head like that, all my thoughts will cease. Besides, I really moved myself when I and my sadness regarded the blanket that I had thrown back in the morning. I will prove to you that my feelings are useful.

HANS
Watch out, if you say it once more, you'll suddenly even believe it. But seriously, I've never heard of a mad businessman. Only the other-directed find themselves ominous. But you're incapable of being at odds with the world. And if you are, you manage to make a profit at it.

QUITT
You're becoming schematic, Hans.

HANS
Because I'm a compulsive talker.

KILB
Ask him about his parents. His father was an itinerant actor. His mother made dolls which she couldn't sell. Both of them failed to return from a trip around the world. They're supposed to have jumped into a volcano. He's their only child.

QUITT

(*To* HANS) I'm not sick. Let's talk about something more harmless.

(*Pause.*)

KILB

For example, the immortality of the soul?

(*Pause.*)

QUITT

The reason I'm not sick is because I, Hermann Quitt, can be just the way I feel. And I'd like to be the way I feel. I feel like the blues, Hans. (*Pause.*) In any event, sometimes I go somewhere and I think I've come in through the wrong door. Another second and they'll ask me who I am. Or I suddenly stand on an incline in my empty office, see the pencil roll down from the desk top and the papers slide off. Even when I come in here, I often become afraid that I've intruded. Frequently when I look at a familiar object I think: Where's the trick? People I've known for ages I suddenly call by their last name. That's not just an old dream. But I wanted to talk about something else. (*Pause.* KILB *raises his hand.* QUITT *has suddenly butted his head against the punching bag.*) What's still possible? What's there left for me to do? Recently I drove through a suburban street where I used to walk every day. Suddenly I saw an old board for posters. In those days I used to look it over and read everything on it. Now the board was nearly empty, only one poster left, an ad for a powdered milk that's long off the market. (*He raises his arms.*) As I drove slowly past, the posters of all the bygone chocolates, toothpastes, and elections passed before my mind's eye, and in this gentle moment of recollection I was overcome by a profound sense of history.

KILB and HANS
(*Simultaneously*) And then you palled it up with your chauffeur?

(*Pause. Honking offstage.*)

QUITT
That's Lutz. He also honks that way at night when he comes home. It's a signal for his wife to turn on the microwave oven. Made in Japan. Go help him with his coat.

(HANS *exits.*)

KILB
(*Steps forward.*) How does that story about your parents go?

QUITT
It's not idiotic enough. I once dreamed I was losing my hair. Whereupon someone told me that I was afraid of becoming impotent. But perhaps it only meant that I was afraid of losing my hair.

KILB
But why are you afraid of losing your hair? What does that mean? Besides, I caught sight of you recently. You were sitting on a bench by the river, rather absentmindedly engrossed in nature.

QUITT
Absentmindedly?

KILB
You hadn't even wiped the pigeon shit off the bench. Besides, experience tells me that the contemplation of nature is the first sign of a waning sense of reality. And your eyelids scarcely blinked, like a child's.

QUITT

Oh, go on, go on. It's beautiful to hear a story about oneself.

KILB

I went to have lunch. Steak and French fries. After all, I exist too.

QUITT

Kilb, I've admired you for a long time. I like your ruthlessness. That time when you brought an effigy of me to the stockholders' meeting and hung it on the lectern! And had yourself carried bodily out of the hall! I envy you too. Next to you I feel constricted, caught inside my skin, and notice how limited I am. I can tell you this now because it's just the two of us.

(KILB *draws* QUITT *forward by both ears and smacks a kiss on his lips.* QUITT *gives him a kick.*)

KILB

So as to re-establish the previous state of affairs. (*He retreats.*)

(*Simultaneously* HANS *leads* LUTZ, VON WULLNOW, *and* KOERBER-KENT *into the room.* KOERBER-KENT, *a businessman-priest, represents a Catholic-owned company; he is dressed in a suit, but wears the collar of his profession.*)

LUTZ

(*To his colleagues*) As I said, we weren't the first ones. We just observed them in the beginning, let them overextend themselves; then we got the green light from our overseas affiliates, tackled them, and down they went. He of course tried to bluff us, but we were on to him long ago. We let him twist in the wind a while longer and then we bagged him.

(*They laugh, each in his own way.*)

VON WULLNOW

(*To* QUITT) Quite something, that bike out there leaning against your fence. My father once gave me one almost like it, together with my first pair of knickers. They don't do work like that any more nowadays. Instead of selling you a bike, they dress it up like a machine, with speedometer and horn. And a machine of course is allowed to wear out more quickly than a simple bike. It is also characteristic of machines that they become obsolete. A bike wouldn't. Do you ride it to work? (QUITT *points to* KILB.) I wondered straight off why it was so dirty.

LUTZ

I'll take his arms. Who'll take the legs?

QUITT

And if we trip, the dragon seed falls out of his mouth. And the new Adam leaps to his feet.

KOERBER-KENT

He doesn't bother me. I find him entertaining. He reminds me of some dark urge inside myself. Besides, he doesn't really mean it. He can't help it, that's all. Ever since we had a chat, just the two of us, I believe him.

LUTZ

It's easy to believe someone if it's just the two of you. I believe anyone if it's just the two of us. But I get nothing out of it. That's why I try not to be alone with anyone. It falsifies the facts.

VON WULLNOW

He has no sense of honor, that s.o.b. He reminds me of an old nag we used to have at home. He pissed every time he stepped from his stall out on the pavement. It made such a wonderful splashing sound. He moved through the world with his joint dangling. And look how bowlegged he is. And the part in the middle of his hair—which isn't really centered. The threadbare fly, the pointy-toed shoes, that's no way to live!

KOERBER-KENT
Von Wullnow, you're wasting your time. There's no insulting him. Your elaborate insults only increase his self-esteem. Let's sit down and begin. I have to prepare a sermon today.

LUTZ
What are you going to preach on?

KOERBER-KENT
About the fact that death makes all men equal. Even us.

VON WULLNOW
(*Indicating* KILB.) He'd like that. But now—should he hear everything?

LUTZ
But we're not going to say anything that no one besides us should hear, are we?

(*Pause. The businessmen laugh.* KILB *is playing with his tongue in his mouth.* HANS *leaves. The businessmen sit down on a set of matching chairs and sofa.*)

VON WULLNOW
Are you standing comfortably, Kilb? We're only human, after all. (*The businessmen laugh again.* QUITT'S WIFE *appears. She looks at all of them, then walks diagonally through the room and disappears.* To KOERBER-KENT) Do you as a priest also employ female help in your enterprises?

KOERBER-KENT
How do you mean?

VON WULLNOW

I was just thinking about the fact that *you* aren't married, neither happily nor at all.

KOERBER-KENT

No, we can't marry.

VON WULLNOW

I didn't mean it that way.

QUITT

I don't understand your allusions.

VON WULLNOW

But you understand that they are allusions?

LUTZ

(*Distracting them.*) Of course, women are cheaper. But you have to be careful. Every month a few of them pull a fast one on us.

KOERBER-KENT

By pilfering inventory?

LUTZ

No, by becoming pregnant. Scarcely have they started work when they turn up with child—not out of passion, mind you, but out of cold calculation; and we have to pay the maternity benefits.

VON WULLNOW

One shouldn't always be talking about the good old days, but things *were* different in the past. You didn't even need to talk about the good old days then. Everyone was one big happy family in my grandfather's shop. They didn't work for my father, they worked for the shop, and that also meant for themselves—at least that's the feeling you got, and that's what mattered. Anyway, our system is the only one in which it is possible to work for oneself. It's incredible how strong my sense of solidarity was with my workers. It cut through all class differences and thresholds of natural feeling when they made their work easier for themselves by singing songs or urging each other on during particularly difficult jobs, with original chants which, incidentally, should be collected before they are forgotten altogether. Today they get the work over and done with, mutely and indifferently, that's all. Their thoughts are somewhere else, nothing creative any more, no imagination. I must say I admire our imports from the South. They're alive during their work, are happy to be together. Work is still part of their life for them. Moreover, in the good old days the workers used to take pride in their products; when they went for their Sunday walks they proudly pointed out to their children anything in the vicinity made by their own hands. Nowadays, most children haven't the faintest idea what their parents do at work.

KILB

Why, do you want them to point out the bolt in the car which their father personally screwed in, or the stick of margarine Mother wrapped herself?

VON WULLNOW

I don't have my cane with me. I refuse to touch you with my bare hands.

KOERBER-KENT

I recently had my library repapered. Of course, I helped with the work, and then I noticed the lack of enthusiasm with which the paper hangers were working, despite the fact that I was paying better than minimum wages. Why is it, I asked them, that you can't develop any passion for your work even though you are paid for it? The good souls didn't have any answer to that one.

VON WULLNOW
Typical.

(KILB *clipping his fingernails in the meantime.*)

KOERBER-KENT
They only think of the money. They've got nothing in their minds except bread and broads, as I always put it. Instead of enrolling in evening courses or absorbing our cultural heritage, they spend their wages on refrigerators, crystal, and knickknacks. Since they no longer have any respect for the public good—not to use a religious word in this circle—they have become possessed by the devil of personal happiness, as I sometimes say jokingly. And yet there's no way for them to be personally happy without considering the public good. You're scarcely born and already you're pushing into the revolving door of the here and now and can't push your way back out, I always say. The paper wraps the stone, consumption cracks the character.

VON WULLNOW
A story. No sermon without a little story, right? I know my rhetoric. Which, incidentally, is another art that has gone to the dogs among us . . . I was walking through the supermarket.

QUITT
You in a supermarket?

VON WULLNOW
Mine, of course. But I wanted to tell a story.

QUITT
Von Wullnow, the supermarket baron, that's news.

VON WULLNOW
I had to invest, taxes forced us to. I don't have to explain
that to you. And besides, a big chain is just the right market
for some of our products. That way we have our own outlets
and don't need to discount to the retailers.

QUITT
"Harald Count von Wullnow Supermarkets."

VON WULLNOW
We called them Miller-Markets. Anyway, when I went to
inspect one of them, I couldn't help noticing a woman who
made herself conspicuous by standing around a long time
with an empty shopping cart. I watched her and wondered
to myself, because, aside from the furtive glances she was
casting about, she seemed almost ladylike. Suddenly she
came up to me and said softly, Do you think they still have
the giant-size detergent on sale that was advertised last week?
Too bad, I thought afterward. She was just my shirt size, I
liked her layout. But to lose one's dignity over a consumer
article like that! I felt quite ashamed for the person.

(KILB *has placed his hands underneath his armpits and is
producing farting noises.*)

LUTZ
All I have to say against the consumers is that they aren't
informed. Why don't they read the business sections in their
papers which publicize the *Good Housekeeping* tests? Why
don't they join the consumer councils? No wonder they can't
tell the products apart. Did you ever watch the faces of housewives during a sale? A mass of mindless, dehumanized, panic-
stricken grimaces that don't even perceive each other any

more, staring hypnotically at objects. No logic, no brains, nothing but the seething, stinking subconscious. A happening at the zoo, gentlemen. No awareness, no life, no feeling for quality. I know whereof I speak.

KILB
(*Interrupts them.*) Fire!

QUITT
(*Ignores him.*) And whereof are you speaking?

LUTZ
You know very well. We stopped production just now. Our quality product had no chance against your mass-produced one. Your brand is a household name, even our packaging, a three-dimensional picture on a hexagonal cover, was too revolutionary. Consumers are conservative, their curiosity about progress is fly-by-night. That was our first fire—I mean fiasco. (*Looks at* KILB.)

QUITT
When your product came on the market, I immediately put ours on the steal-me list.

KOERBER-KENT
Please explain.

QUITT
The steal-me list is a full-page ad which we publish once a week in the major newspapers. It lists the ten products of ours that are shoplifted with the greatest frequency. Simultaneously we send this list as posters to the trade. There they construct a kind of altar display of the listed objects and the poster with the legend SHOPLIFTERS' HIT PARADE is hung above it. This boosts sales. I immediately put my product at the top of the list and left it there, until Lutz gave up. I must say

I've grown fond of it in the meantime and look at it in its plain square package with genuine affection. Still, I'm going to stop production on it.

LUTZ
What do you mean?

QUITT
It was a losing proposition for a long time. I just didn't want you to get a swelled head.

VON WULLNOW
Marvelous, Quitt! That's the old school spirit, but I can see now how important it is that we reach an agreement in time.

QUITT
Otherwise why would you be here?

VON WULLNOW
Businessmen are people who get things moving, as Schumpeter says. Let's oil the machinery of the world.

KILB
Someone's coming.

VON WULLNOW
(*Doesn't hear him.*) This is an important day. For the first time we want to give up our atomization. We've been lonely long enough. We planned in loneliness, in sad isolation we watched the market, helplessly each of us set his price by himself, hoping for the best. Despising everything that was alien, each of us on his little island watched the other's advertising campaigns. We did not recognize our mutual needs, were even proud of our individualism. That has to change; we can't go on like this.

(PAULA TAX *hurriedly enters.*)

QUITT
I was just thinking of you, Paula.

PAULA
And?

QUITT
Nothing bad.

VON WULLNOW
Have a seat. (*To the others*) I always find it embarrassing to say to a woman, Sit down. (*To* PAULA) All of us were thinking of you. Even the Vicar-General, I think?

KOERBER-KENT
(*Jokingly*) Now I know why I felt the whole time as if a door had been left open somewhere.

KILB
Your signet ring is tarnished, Monsignore.

KOERBER-KENT
Continue, my friend. (KILB *remains silent.*) He's never got more than one sentence in him. The habit of quick interjections has ruined him.

(PAULA *has sat down. She is still wearing riding clothes.* QUITT'S WIFE *comes in again. She pretends she is looking for something.* PAULA *loosens her scarf and shakes her hair.* QUITT'S WIFE *stomps her feet. As she walks on, the heel of her shoe gets caught in a crack in the floor. She hops backward, slips back into the shoe, and tries to walk out with measured steps.* KILB *barks after her and she disappears with a scream.*)

QUITT

Perhaps the reason for the nausea is that only a minute ago you could have held an entirely different opinion of the matter, and in that case the story would have taken an entirely different turn.

PAULA

You look at me as if I should ask, What does this mean?

QUITT

Please remind me later that I must still explain something to you.

PAULA
When?

QUITT
Later.

LUTZ

I don't want to be pushy. There's a lot at stake today. I wouldn't have been able to fall asleep last night without my autogenic training. I usually think of the ocean when that happens, but even that sparkled for a long time like freshly mashed spinach from my new freezer package, and the moon above had been crossed out with a felt pen and a smaller one circled in beside it.

VON WULLNOW

All right, let's get down to business. I assume, if not our conversation, then what we mean by it is ears only. In any event, you have my word of honor. (*He takes a look around.*) The Vicar-General swears on this, doesn't he? Lutz promises, or no? And Quitt? Nods. Mrs. Tax's thoughts are still nudging her horse with her thighs. And our guest of honor? (*He nods briefly toward* KILB.)

QUITT
Hans.

(HANS *appears at once, frisks* KILB, *shakes his head—"no microphone"—and withdraws again.* KILB *thereupon takes his stool and sits down with the others, assumes the pose of a kibitzer.*)

VON WULLNOW
We're no sharks. But we've learned that free enterprise is a dog-eat-dog business. Public opinion regards us as monsters belching cigar smoke. And in the often so poetically quoted moments of those overly long cross-country trips we see ourselves like that: we've become what once we didn't want to become at any price. Don't shake your head, Vicar-General. You know that's not the way I mean it. No, we aren't just the bad guys in a game: we really are bad. Even as a gourmet, my face has slowly but surely become less and less soulful—although for a long time I hoped for the opposite. Just take a look at your colleagues business-lunching in the three-star restaurants, Lutz: their jowls register a lifelong sellout. A lifelong circus, not just twice a year like the housewives. Still, it is premature undialectical impressionism, as Mrs. Tax would surely say, trying to dump on us. After all, we didn't become monsters because we relished it. My primal experience is the thought: There's no such thing as a human being who becomes inhuman of his own accord. That's what I tell myself whenever I have to put myself together again after having done something I actually abhor in my heart of hearts.

QUITT
What you're trying to say is that it's futile to try to enlarge the market any further by means of price wars.

LUTZ

(*Glances at* KILB.) Not like that. Everyone should be able to translate it into his own terms.

QUITT

Competition is a game. Fighting is childish. Together we can underbid the small fry until they long to live from dividends. Not force, but the gentle law of displacement. When I was a child I would sometimes quietly sit down on something that someone else wanted, and absentmindedly whistle a song to myself.

KOERBER-KENT

You're not at confession here, Quitt.

QUITT

To the point: first of all: there are too many products, the market has become opaque. Who is producing too much? One of us? Perish the thought. Who then? They, of course. We're going to make the market transparent again. Second: now there are no longer too many products but too many units of the same product. The refrigeration plants are bursting with butter, I read at breakfast today. Is our supply too large? No, demand is too low, and that's the catch we live off of. Third of all: is demand too low because prices are too high? Of course. And prices are too high because wages are too high, right? So we are going to have to pay lower wages. But how? By having the work done more cheaply somewhere else. Say, "Mauritius represents an excellent labor market. The plantations have accustomed the population to hard work for generations. The nimble Asiatic fingers have become skilled and are a proven value." Therefore, we will be able to claim that our merchandise is a bigger bargain. That's the biggest drawing card. Besides, imagine that all goods will bear the legend: "Made in Mauritius." I remember the yearning such labels used to instill in me as a child. Why shouldn't they exert the same effect on our beloved consumers? In any event, demand will rise and we will match up our prices again. Fourth: from time to time we take a walk through the forest by ourselves so as to feel like human beings. Fifth: (*To* von wullnow) All this time I've felt the irresistible urge to wipe off your wet mouth. (*He wipes off* von wullnow's *mouth with a handkerchief. To* kilb) Repeat what I've said just now.

(*Pause.*)

KILB
(*Moves his lips, falters, tries again, shakes his head. He hops on his stool toward* quitt.) Anyway, it sounded logical. As logical as this here. (*He tugs at both his ears and his tongue sticks out of his mouth, grabs his chin, and the tongue slips back inside. The businessmen meanwhile have exchanged significant glances.*)

LUTZ
So we're celebrating already?

QUITT
I'm not finished yet.

KOERBER-KENT
What were you playing just now? It was just a game, wasn't it? Because in reality you are—

QUITT
(*Interrupts him.*) Yes, but only in reality. (*To* von wullnow) And you are speechless?

VON WULLNOW
I'm just getting used to you again. Perhaps you're just one of those people who like to squeeze other people's pimples.

QUITT

(*Strikes his forehead histrionically.*) True, I was carried away by something. But now I'm normal again.

VON WULLNOW

It passed so quickly I've already forgotten it. I was brushed by a bat. Did something happen? Besides, you haven't finished yet.

QUITT

What is important is that from now on none of us does anything without the other. When I buy raw materials without informing you of my source, that's treason. When Lutz brings a new product on the market to corner a share of the turf, that's treason. If the Vicar-General pays his female labor a lower scale than we do, because they are devout farm girls, and depresses prices, that's treason. If you, Paula, let your workers share in the profits and have to raise prices all by yourself, that's treason. (*To* VON WULLNOW) That's the way you want it, isn't it?

VON WULLNOW

Mrs. Tax would probably pose the counterquestion: But what if I let them share because I find it reasonable—say, to increase production?

QUITT

(*To* PAULA, *as if she had answered for herself*) It's not treason as long as you don't raise your prices without first consulting us. And as long as you and I have the same habits, you can't betray me. And now the champagne, Hans.

(*A cork pops backstage.* HANS *appears at once, carrying a tray with champagne glasses and a bottle which is still smoking. The ceremony of pouring the champagne.* QUITT *points ironically to the quality of the champagne and glasses, for example:* "*Dom Pérignon 1935, Biedermeier glasses, hand-blown, notice the irregularities in the glass." The group rises to its feet, clinks glasses, drinks quietly, looking into each other's eyes.* KILB *has not gotten up. While the others are drinking he briefly laughs a few times without the others paying him any heed. He pulls out his knife, turns it back and forth, and lets it fall mumblety-peg fashion to the floor. They look at him without interest. He puts the knife away and plays a little on his harmonica.* HANS *has already left with the tray.* KILB *gets up and spits at the feet of each person, one after the other. In front of* PAULA *he uses his hand to pull out his chin, simultaneously sticking out his behind. The rest continue to regard him benignly. Suddenly he picks up* LUTZ *and the priest, who don't object, one after the other, and puts them down somewhere else. He crisscrosses the stage. In passing, he kicks them lightly on the backs of their knees so that their legs give a little, except for the last one. He offers* PAULA *his thigh, Harpo Marx fashion, which she holds and then lets drop again; he makes an exception of* QUITT, *only casting sidelong glances at him. Now he has also begun to speak.*)

KILB
And I? Is it my job to take care of the entertainment? Am I the critter whose ears are allowed to hear everything? Or the poodle in front of whom you lie down naked in bed? I can drag you across your beautiful lawns with my teeth. I'll stuff the gaps in your beautiful whole sentences with pus. I'll cram your spray-deodorized private parts into Baggies. You singe the fluff off slaughtered chickens with a candle. In Switzerland they say "chicken skin" instead of "goose bumps." Enjoy! Enjoy! I always speak this calmly, dear lady. Here, you've dropped your Charmin. (*He pulls out a strip of toilet paper and places it over her arm; she smiles, unimpressed.*) If you ever catch fire it will be me who wraps you in blankets until you choke to death. And when you all freeze to death I'll sit

beside you cracking my knuckles. Diabolical, don't you agree? (*More and more embarrassed*) Let yourselves be conjured up out of your personal hedgerows, you, the bewitched of the business world, a free man stands before you, a model, a picture-book figure. (*He slaps his hands together, slaps his thighs and the soles of his shoes like a folk dancer, only more slowly and awkwardly.*) Let's swing a little! Action! Lights! A little circus atmosphere! Not just words against which the brain is defenseless anyway! Conserve your vocal chords! More body language! (*He picks up a champagne glass and lets it drop somewhat helplessly, makes a vain reflex movement to catch it, which he tries to overplay.*) And don't stand around like a bunch of stiffs! Anyway, far too statuesque! Move. You will be recognized by your movements. Let's celebrate. (*He dances* PAULA *a few steps farther across the stage, then stops in front of her. He starts unbuttoning her blouse . . . He encourages himself by beating his fists together and blowing into the hollow of his hands. In between he sticks his hands into his armpits as if they were freezing. No one stops him. Sidelong glances at* QUITT. QUITT *watches him attentively as well as remotely, almost impatiently.* KILB *tugs the blouse out of the riding britches, somewhat indecisively.* PAULA *merely smiles. He steps back as if he were giving up, performs another pathetic slapping gesture without really slapping his hands together. Suddenly* QUITT *leaps forward, seizes* KILB's *hand, and wants to use it to tear off* PAULA's *blouse himself.* KILB *resists.* QUITT's WIFE *enters, watches with interest.* QUITT *lets go of* KILB *and tears off the blouse himself.* PAULA *crosses her arms in front of her breasts without undue hurry.* QUITT's WIFE *leaves.* QUITT *places another champagne glass in* KILB's *hand, simultaneously takes the other glasses into his fist, and smashes them, one after the other, on the floor, repeating* KILB's *words—"Enjoy! enjoy!"— while doing so . . . nudges him in the side until* KILB, *too, drops his glass, somewhat indecisively.* QUITT *walks from one person to the other and spits into each face; lifts up a splinter of glass and attacks* KILB *with it, throws the splinter away, and puts* KILB *into a headlock; leads him back and forth like this and butts his head against the others. In the headlock, trying to free himself*) You misunderstood me, Quitt. There's no method to your madness. It is unaesthetic, vulgar, formless. But worst of all, it is unmusical, has neither melody nor rhythm. That wasn't how we planned it. Don't you understand a joke? Can't you distinguish between ritual and reality any more? Know your limits, Quitt.

QUITT
(*While pushing him into a chair and dragging him offstage on it*) Until now you have lived off the fact that I have my limits, you phony. Now show me my limits, you model of the independent life. (*Far upstage he tips him out of sight and comes back.*)

(PAULA *walks off with measured steps.* HANS *reappears with a dustpan and whisk broom. The others are cleaning themselves. Everyone begins to smile.* QUITT *does not smile.* HANS *sweeps the splinters together.* PAULA *returns dressed and smiles also, with closed lips.*)

VON WULLNOW
I believe he's finally learned his lesson.

KOERBER-KENT
He'll never learn anything, He's got no memory. The jack-in-the-box merely uses the floor to propel himself. He doesn't forget because he doesn't remember anything. The horsefly lands on the very spot it's just been shooed away from. He doesn't think backward and forward like us who have a sense of history—as Mrs. Tax might say—he only has a good nose. I would call him a mere animal, an involuntary, fidgeting animal. The sparrows in the field, not by living, but by being

lived, are the divine principle. I can see him now on his bicycle animalistically rushing down the tree-lined avenues.

QUITT

Don't always look at me when you speak; I can't listen to you that way.

VON WULLNOW

It's a pity that there are no more tree-lined avenues. How sweet, for instance, the memory of the manor house at dawn—the house at the vanishing point of the two rows of chestnut trees, the windows reflecting darkly, only the dormers of the servants' quarters already lighted up; a hedgehog rustles in the dry leaves at our feet, the special stagnant air of that time of day when the sick go into themselves and die willingly, and a chestnut suddenly thuds down and bursts on the gun on our shoulder while we have turned around for one last look at our parents' house before we stalk crosscountry to our hunting ground. Yes, a delicate being, our minority stockholder, as delicate as a thief when it comes to opening a drawer, as delicate as a murderer when it comes to handling a knife.

LUTZ

Von Wullnow, your language is so elevated it makes me hesitate to tell my joke now.

VON WULLNOW

I order you to. You've been looking all this time as if you had something to get off your chest.

LUTZ

Two people love each other. They make love so rapidly, the way you sometimes devour a slice of bread with honey on it. When they are finished—(*Glances at* PAULA.) Oh, pardon me.

VON WULLNOW

Mrs. Tax isn't listening anyway. And besides, she's above that sort of thing. She'd probably consider our dirty jokes as proof of our commercialized sexuality, wouldn't you? Go on.

LUTZ

—the man gets up at once. Oh, says the woman, you've scarcely finished and you're already leaving? And that's supposed to be love? Look, the man replies, I counted to ten, didn't I?

(*There's either brief laughter or there isn't.* VON WULLNOW *is already in the process of departing with* LUTZ *and* KOERBER-KENT—*only* HANS, *who is still sweeping up broken glass, giggles, kneeling on the floor. The gentlemen turn around toward him; he gets up and proceeds out in front of them, giggling.*)

VON WULLNOW

Quitt, we trust you as you trust us. Forget your superannuated sensitivity. Sensitive for me is a word I only associate with condoms.

QUITT

(*To* PAULA) Aren't you leaving?

PAULA

I was to remind you that you still wanted to explain something to me.

QUITT

I merely *wished* you would stay, now you can go. (*Pause.* PAULA *sits down again. Pause.*) I noticed how I happened to think of you disgustingly by chance. One minute before and all I could have attached to you was your name. Suddenly there was something conspicuous about you. I wanted to get up and grab you between the legs.

PAULA

Are you speaking about me or about a thing?

QUITT

(*Laughs briefly. Pause.*) Just now I almost said: About you, you thing. Something seems to want to slip out of me today, something I'm afraid of but which still tantalizes me. You know the stories about laughing at funerals. Once I sat opposite a woman I didn't know. We looked into each other's eyes until I felt hot. Suddenly she stuck out her tongue at me, not just mockingly, a little between her lips, but all the way to the root, with the whole face a gruesome grimace—as though she wanted to stick herself out at me. Ever since then I've felt like doing something like that myself. Usually I manage to do it only in my head, for just a moment. It starts with my wanting to undo someone's shoelaces who's walking by or pulling a hair out of his nose, and stops with the urge to unzip my fly in company.

PAULA

Shouldn't we talk about our arrangement instead?

QUITT

But I'm finally beginning to enjoy talking. I am speaking now. Before, my lips just moved. I had to strain my muscles to enunciate properly. My whole chin ached, the cheeks became numb. Now I know what I am saying.

PAULA

Are you Catholic?

QUITT

Why! You're actually listening to me!

speaks as if she wants to avoid speaking of something else.)
My workers should never see me like this. Normally, I buy
my clothes ready-to-wear, I even feel good in them. By the
way, it occurred to me before that we should also plan our
advertising together from now on. I would like to go on the
basis that we don't generate any artificial needs but only
awaken the natural ones of which people aren't conscious
yet. Most people don't even know their needs. Advertising,
insofar as it describes a product, is only another word for
consciousness-raising. What we should avoid is advertising
which is inappropriate to its product because it creates mis-
conceptions among the consumers about the nature of the
product. That would be the very deception or simulation of
something that isn't there which we are always accused of.
But our products exist and their very existence makes them
rational—otherwise we, as rational beings, would not have
had them produced in a rational manner from rational raw
materials by rational people. And if our advertisements don't
lie but only provide an exact description of our rational products, then the advertising will be just as rational. Take a look
at the socialist states. They have no irrational products—and
still they advertise, because the rational needs advertising
most of all. That's what transmits the idea of what is rational.
For me advertising is the only materialistic poetry. As an
anthropomorphic system it endears us to the objects from
which we have been alienated by ideology. It animates the
world of goods and humanizes them, so that we can feel at
home with them. I can't tell you how deeply touched I am
when I read on an old fire wall in giant letters PEPSI-COLA
HITS THE SPOT. When I see a detergent container in front of
a rising sun, it blows my mind. Today, twenty years later,
they simply gave the same product the sappy designation
IT'S THE PEPSI GENERATION, and my mind goes blank. When
I'm feeling unproductive, I look at ads in magazines, it makes
my mood seem ridiculous; so advertising is also a form of
consolation, but of a concrete, rational kind, as distinct from

bourgeois obscurantist poetry. And think with how much more dignity and how much more progressively the copywriters can work than the poets! While the poets in their isolation conjure up something vague, the copywriters, working as an efficient team, describe the definite. Indeed, they are the only truly creative ones—they think something they had no idea about beforehand. Incidentally, we noticed recently what was wrong with the slogan for one of our products. It contained the phrase "a level tablespoon" and the product didn't sell. Finally it occurred to one member of the team to substitute the word "heaping" for small. Instead of "level tablespoon" we used "a heaping teaspoon," and suddenly sales increased by almost 100 percent.

(HANS *enters during the last sentence and turns on the light.*)

QUITT
(*To* HANS) We don't need any light.

(HANS *turns off the light and leaves.*)

PAULA
I can hear my wristwatch ticking.

QUITT
You should be able to afford a noiseless watch. But that probably is an heirloom, not just any old watch. So please try to remember. (*Pause.*) Or don't try to remember—as you please.

PAULA
If you tell a child who is singing to itself: Very nice, go on singing! it will stop singing. But if you say: Stop! it will go on singing.

QUITT
There are women who—

PAULA
Stop it, nothing can come of that.

QUITT
There are women you can't touch because if you did you
would be desecrating an heirloom. A necklace, then, has a
story which makes every caress of the neck a mere after-
thought. Everything about the woman is so complete that
every experience you share with her only reminds her of
something in her past. Whatever you tell her, she immediately interrupts you with this introverted nodding of the head.
She is untouchable, inside and out. She is so full of memories.
The most mysterious, delicately stuttering impulse immediately evokes a doppelgänger who has already made the impulse crystal-clear to the woman. You begin to understand
sex killers: only the slitting open of the belly provides him
with the attention every individual deserves. You can't run
your hands through a hooker's hair—so that her hairdo won't
get messed up.

PAULA
It's just as you say it is. But why is it like that? Who is
responsible for that? And who makes sure that it stays that
way? And who profits by it? Instead of naming the causes,
you make fun of their appearances. And precisely that happens to be one of the causes. To describe pure appearances is
a man's kind of joke. Von Wullnow would say that I would
say: undialectical impressionism.

QUITT
And you: because you've got so many causes on your mind,
you forget to bother with the appearances. Instead of appearances, you see nothing but causes. And when you elimi-

nate the causes so as to change the appearances, they have already changed so that you have to eliminate entirely different causes. And if you look at me now, please become aware of me for once and not my causes.

PAULA

You have a beautiful tie pin. Your shirt is so new that one can still see the pinholes. Your grinding jaws manifest will power. Your delicate hands might be those of a pianist. One of your earlobes has dried shaving cream on it. And while you behave animalistically, the creases on your pants give you away.

(QUITT *gets up and pulls* PAULA *toward him. She wraps her arms exaggeratedly around him and also puts one leg around his hip, throws back her head, and sighs derisively. He lets go of her at once and walks away. She walks backward. They pursue each other alternately for a short time. Then they walk around by themselves, finally stop.*)

QUITT

Please stop being conceptual. I once gave someone a present, some chocolate for his child. The chocolate was wrapped in small squares, each one with a picture of a different fairy-tale motif. Oh, the father said disappointedly, it's not a puzzle! And then he said: That's it, deprivation of the imagination by the chocolate manufacturers. When he said that, I suddenly stood very distantly beside him and felt radically alone. I looked down at the floor in utter loneliness. So, please stop.

PAULA

But you were the one who started it.

QUITT

Do you see that nail sticking out of the wall there?

PAULA
Yes.

QUITT
It's long, isn't it?

PAULA
Very long.

QUITT
And how thick is your head?

(*Pause.*)

PAULA
Perhaps I should turn on the light after all.

(*Pause.*)

QUITT
Today the doorbell rang. Because I was curious who it was, I went to open the door myself. It was only the eggman, whom the so-called estate sends around from house to house once a week. He always comes at the same time. I'd forgotten. "Can't you be someone else for once?" I wanted to scream.

(*Pause.*)

PAULA
And what if *I* were someone else?

(QUITT *takes one step toward her. She does not step back.*)

QUITT
And recently I saw a silent film. No music had been dubbed in, so it was almost completely quiet in the theater. Only

now and then when something funny happened a few scattered children laughed and stopped again at once. Suddenly I had a sense of death. The feeling was so strong that I yanked my legs far apart and spread my fingers. What social conditions can you use to explain that? Does this syndrome already bear someone's name? If so, whose?

PAULA
I can't explain it to you by social conditions. It is unconditionally yours and can't be emulated. As a social factor it's not worth mentioning. The masses have other worries.

QUITT
But which will pass.

PAULA
Yes, because the conditions will pass too.

QUITT
And then the masses will perhaps have my worries, which do not pass.

(WIFE *appears with a magazine in her hand.*)

WIFE
Austrian dramatist, dead, seven letters?

QUITT
Nestroy.

WIFE
No.

QUITT
Across or down?

WIFE
Across.

QUITT
Raimund.

WIFE
Of course. (*Exits.*)

(*Pause.*)

PAULA
The watch—it isn't an heirloom. (*Pause.*) Is that still too conceptual?

QUITT
Now I won't tell you what I'm thinking.

PAULA
And what are you thinking?

QUITT
It's kind of you to ask. But why don't you ask me of your own volition? I yearn to be questioned by you. Do I have to bang my head against the floor to make you ask about me? (*He throws himself on the floor and actually bangs his head a few times against it, then stands up at once and steps up to* PAULA.) I would like to snap at the world now and swallow it, that's how inaccessible everything seems to me. And I too am inaccessible, I twist away from everything. Every event I could possibly experience slowly but surely transforms itself back into lifeless nature, where I no longer play a role. I can stand before it as I do before you and I am back in prehistory without human beings. I imagine the ocean, the fire-spewing volcanoes, the primordial mountains on the horizon, but the conception has nothing to do with me. I don't even appear

dimly within it as a premonition. When I look at you now,
I see you only as you are, and as you are entirely without me,
but not as you were or could be with me; that is inhuman.

PAULA
Excuse me, but I can't concentrate any longer. (*She takes a
step, so that their bodies touch.*) So what were you thinking?

(*Pause.*)

QUITT
You know it anyway.

PAULA
Perhaps. But I'd like to hear you say it.

QUITT
Now I feel strong enough not to tell you any more.

PAULA
(*Steps back.*) We are alone.

QUITT
I am alone and you are alone, not we. I would not want to
transpose the "we" of our deal to you and me at this moment.

PAULA
Isn't this moment, too, part of our deal?

QUITT
Don't you get out of your box even for a second?

PAULA
Your impatience is what keeps me boxed in.

QUITT
(*Flings her to the floor. She lies there, supports herself on one elbow. Then she gets up.*) How gracefully you get back on your feet!

PAULA
I'd like to leave now.

QUITT
Hans!

(HANS *appears with a long fur coat over his arm and first walks in the wrong direction.*)

QUITT
Over here. Where did you think you were?

HANS
(*Helps* PAULA *into her coat.*) Always with you, Mr. Quitt. It was bright in the room I just left.

PAULA
Hans, you're good at helping people into their coats.

HANS
Mrs. Quitt has the same one.

PAULA
(*To* QUITT) I would like to tell you something about myself, Quitt, just like this, without being asked to. And note that, for the first time, I'm speaking about myself. After your wife left I slowly exhaled. And while exhaling . . . please don't laugh.

QUITT
I'm not laughing.

PAULA
While exhaling . . . please don't laugh.

QUITT
Another second and I will.

PAULA
(*Loudly*) As I exhaled, love set in. (*She leaves.*)

QUITT
(*To* HANS) Don't say anything.

HANS
I'm not saying anything.

(QUITT's WIFE *enters, turns on mild indirect lighting, and sits down. She gives* HANS *a signal to leave.*)

QUITT
Nobody's cleaned up. (HANS *proceeds to dust. To his* WIFE) And what did you do all day?

WIFE
You saw what I did: I went in and out and back and forth.

QUITT
And what was it like in town?

WIFE
People respected me.

(HANS *leaves.*)

QUITT
Was there anything new?

WIFE
I stole this blouse.

QUITT
The main thing is not to get caught. Anything else?

WIFE
I stopped here and there and then walked on. Why don't you sit down too?

QUITT
You don't look well.

(*Pause.*)

WIFE
Yes, but at least it's already evening. (*She gets up and walks out quickly.*)

(QUITT *sits down even before she's gone. He remains alone for a while. The silhouette of the city is completely illuminated in the meantime.* HANS *returns with a book.* QUITT *looks up.*)

HANS
It's me, still.

QUITT
Tell me, Hans, what's your life actually like?

(HANS *sits down.*)

HANS
I knew what you would say the moment you opened your mouth. But I couldn't interrupt you at that point. So let's forget it.

(*Pause.*)

QUITT
Stop looking me in the eye.

HANS
I do that whenever I'm at a loss how to please you.

QUITT
Tell me about yourself.

HANS
What do you mean?

QUITT
Don't you understand, I am curious to know your story. How do *you* behave when you would like to speak but can only scream? Don't you sometimes get so tired that you can only imagine everything flat on the ground? Doesn't it also sometimes happen to you that when you think of your relationship to others you only see heavy wet rags lying around everywhere? Now tell me about yourself.

HANS
You mention me.
Yourself you mean.

(*Pause.*)

QUITT
Why does my itty-bitty mind go yakking so affectedly into the big wide world? And can't help itself? (*Screams*) And doesn't want it any differently? I am important. I am important. I am important. Incidentally, why don't you look me in the eye now?

HANS
Because there's nothing new to see there.

(*Pause.*)

QUITT
Please read to me.

HANS
(*Sits down and reads.*) " 'I shall have to let you go after all,'
his uncle said one day at the end of the midday meal, just as
a magnificent thunderstorm was breaking, sending the rustling rain like diamond missiles down into the lake, so that
it twitched and seethed and heaved. Victor made no reply
whatever but listened for what else would come. 'Everything
is futile in the end,' his uncle started up again in a slow
drawn-out voice, 'it's futile, youth and old age don't belong
together. The years that could have been used have passed
now, they are lowering down on the other side of the mountains and no power on earth can drag them back to the near
side where cold shadows are already falling.' Victor could not
have been more awed. The venerable old man happened to
be sitting in such a way that the lightning flashes illuminated
his face, and sometimes, in the dusky room, it seemed as
though fire flowed through the man's gray hair and light
trickled across his weatherbeaten face. 'Oh, Victor, do you
know life? Do you know that thing that people call old
age?'—'How could I, Uncle, as I am still so young?'—'True,
you don't know it, and there's no way you could. Life is
boundless as long as you are still young. You always think you
still have a long stretch ahead of you, that you've traveled
only a short way. That's why you put so much off to the next
day, why you put this and that aside, to tackle it later on.
But then when you want to tackle it, it is too late and you
notice that you are old. That is why life is a limitless field if
you look at it from the beginning, and is scarcely two paces
long when you regard it from the end. It is a sparkling thing,
something so beautiful that you feel like plunging into it,
and you feel that it would have to last forever—and old age
is a moth darting in the dusk, fluttering ominously about
our ears. That is why you would like to stretch out your hands

so as not to have to leave, because you have missed so much. When an aged man stands on a mountain of achievements, what good is it to him? I have done much, all sorts of things, and have nothing from it. Everything turns to dust in a moment if you haven't built an existence that outlasts your coffin. The man who has sons, nephews, and grandsons around him in his old age will often become a thousand years old. Then the same many-sided life persists even when he is gone, life continues just the same; yes, you don't even notice that one small segment of this life veered off to the side and never came back any more. With my death everything that I myself have been will disappear.' After these words the old man stopped speaking. He folded his napkin together, as was his custom, rolled it into a cylinder, and shoved it into the silver ring which he kept for the purpose. Then he assembled the various bottles into a certain order, put the cheese and sweetmeats on their plates, and plunged the glass bells over them. Yet of all these objects he took none away from the table, as was his usual habit, but left them standing there and sat before them. Meanwhile, the thunderstorm had passed, with softer flashes and a muted thundering it moved down the far slope of the craggy eastern mountain range, and the sun fought its way back out, gradually filling the room with a lovely fire. At daybreak the next morning Victor took his walking stick into his hand and slung one strap of his satchel over his arm. The spitz, who understood everything, bounded with joy. Breakfast was consumed amid much small talk. 'I'll take you as far as the gate,' the uncle said when Victor had gotten up, had hitched his satchel on his shoulder, and was about to take his leave. The old man had gone into the adjacent room and must have triggered a spring or set off some kind of mechanical contraption; for at that moment Victor heard the rattling of the gate and saw, through the window, how that gate opened slowly by itself. 'Well,' said his uncle while walking out, 'everything is ready,' Victor reached for his walking stick and placed his cap on his head.

The uncle walked down the stairs with him and across the open space in the garden as far as the gate. Neither said a word during their walk. At the gate the uncle stopped. Victor looked at him for a while. Tears shimmered in his bright-colored eyes, testifying to a profound emotion—then he suddenly bent down and vehemently kissed the wrinkled hand. The old man emitted a dull uncanny sound like a sob—and pushed the youth out by the gate. In two hours the latter had reached Attmaning, and as he stepped out from the dark trees toward the town he happened to hear its bells tolling, and never has a sound sounded so sweet to him as this tolling which fell so endearingly upon his ears, a sound he had not heard for so long. The Innkeeper's Alley was filled with the beautiful brown animals of the mountains which the cattle dealers were driving down toward the lowland, and the inn's guest room was full of people since it was market day. It seemed to Victor as if he had been dreaming for a long time and had only now returned to the world. Now that he was back out in the fields of the people, on their highways, part of their merry doings, now that the expanse of gentle rolling hills stretched out wide and endless before him, and the mountains which he had left hovered behind as a blue wreath; now his heart came apart in this great circumambient view and outraced him far, far beyond the distant, scarcely visible line of the horizon . . ."

QUITT

How nice that this armchair has a headrest. (*Pause.*) How much time has passed since then! In those days, in the nineteenth century, even if you didn't have some feeling for the world, there at least existed a memory of a universal feeling, and a yearning. That is why you could replay the feeling and replay it for the others as in this story. And because you could replay the feeling as seriously and patiently and conscientiously as a restorer—the German poet Adalbert Stifter after all was a restorer—that feeling was really produced, perhaps.

In any event, people believed that what was being played there existed, or at least that it was possible. All I actually do is quote; everything that is meant to be serious immediately becomes a joke with me, genuine signs of life of my own slip out of me purely by accident, and they exist only at the moment when they slip out. Afterward then they are— well—where you once used to see the whole, I see nothing but particulars now. Hey, you with your ingrown earlobes! it suddenly slips out of me, and instead of speaking with someone whom I notice, I step on his heels so that his shoe comes off. I would so like to be full of pathos! Von Wullnow, with a couple of women bathing in the nude at sunrise, bawled out nothing but old college songs in the water—that's what's left of him. What slips out of me is only the raw sewage of previous centuries. I lead a businessman's life as camouflage. I go to the telephone as soon as it rings. I talk faster with the car door open behind me. We fix our prices and faithfully stick to our agreements. Suddenly it occurs to me that I am playing something that doesn't even exist, and that's the difference. That's the despair of it! Do you know what I'm going to do? I won't stick to our arrangement. I'm going to ruin their prices and them with it. I'm going to employ my old-fashioned sense of self as a means of production. I haven't had anything of myself yet, Hans. And they are going to cool their hot little heads with their clammy hands, and their heads will grow cold as well. It will be a tragedy. A tragedy of business life, and I will be the survivor. And the investment in the business will be me, just me alone. I will slip out of myself and the raw sewage will sweep them away. There will be lightning and thunder, and the idea will become flesh.

(*There is thunder.*)

HANS
This time
I can find no rhyme.

QUITT
Good night.

(HANS *leaves.* QUITT *drums his fists on his chest and emits Tarzan-like screams. Pause. His* WIFE *comes in and stops in front of him.*)

WIFE
I have something else to say to you.

QUITT
Don't speak to me. I want to get out of myself now. I am now myself and as such I am on speaking terms only with myself.

WIFE
But I would like to say something to you. Please.

(*Pause.*)

QUITT
(*Suddenly very tender*) Then tell me. (*He takes her around the waist, she moves in his embrace.*) Tell me.

WIFE
I . . . where it . . . because . . . hm (*She clears her throat.*) . . . and you . . . isn't it . . . (*She laughs indecisively.*) . . . this and that . . . and autumn . . . like a stone . . . that roaring . . . the Ammonites . . . and the mud on the soles of the shoes . . . (*She puts her hand to her face, and the stage becomes dark.*)

END ACT ONE

Act II

The silhouette of the city. The punching bag has been re-placed by a huge balloon which, almost imperceptibly, is shrinking. A large, slowly melting block of ice with a spot shining on it has replaced the matching sofa and armchairs, a glass trough with dough rising in it somewhere else, also with a spot on it. A piano. A large boulder in the background with phrases slowly and constantly appearing and fading on it: OUR GREATEST SIN—THE IMPATIENCE OF CONCEPTS—THE WORST IS OVER—THE LAST HOPE. *Next to them are children's drawings. The usual stage lighting (which remains the same throughout).*

HANS is lying on an old deck chair, dressed as before, and is asleep. He is mumbling in his sleep and laughs; time passes.

QUITT walks in from behind the wall, rubbing his hands. He executes a little dance step while walking. He whistles to himself.

QUITT

It's been ages since I've whistled! (*He hums. The humming makes him want to talk.*) Hey, Hans! (HANS *leaps up out of his sleep and immediately goes to relieve* QUITT *of the coat which he isn't wearing.*) You can't stop acting the servant even in your sleep, can you? When I was just singing to myself I suddenly couldn't stand being alone any more. (*He regards* HANS.) And now you're already annoying me again. Were you dreaming of me? Oh, forget it, I don't even want to know. (*He whistles again.* HANS *whistles along.*) Stop whistling. It's no fun if you whistle along.

HANS

I dreamed. Really, I was dreaming. The dream was about a pocket calendar with rough and smooth sides. The rough sides were the work days, the smooth ones the days which I have off. I slithered for days on end over calendar pages.

QUITT

Dream on, little dreamer, dream—just as long as you don't interpret your dreams.

HANS

But what if the dream interprets itself—as it did just now?

QUITT

You are talking about yourself—why is that?

HANS

You've infected me.

QUITT

And how?

HANS

By employing your personality—and having success with yourself too. Suddenly I saw that I lacked something. And when I thought about it I realized that I lacked everything. For the first time I didn't just sort of exist for myself, but existed as someone who is comparable, say, with you. I couldn't bear the comparing any more, began to dream, evaluated myself. Incidentally, you just interrupted me and it was important. (*He sits down and closes his eyes. He shakes his head.*) Too bad. It's over. I felt really connected when I was dreaming. (*To* QUITT) I don't want to have to go on shaking my head much longer.

QUITT
It occurs to me I should have gotten you up earlier. Then you wouldn't get ideas like this. So you want to leave me?

HANS
On the contrary, I want to stay forever. I still have much to learn from you.

QUITT
Would you like to be like me?

HANS
I have to be. Recently I've been forcing myself to copy your handwriting. I no longer write with a slant but vertically. That is like standing up after a lifetime of bowing down. But it hurts, too. I also no longer put my hands like this . . . (*Thumbs forward, fingers backward on his hips*) on my hips, but like you do . . . (*Fingers forward, thumbs backward*) That gives me more self-confidence. Or standing up . . . (*He stands up.*) I stand on one leg and play with the other like you. A new sense of leisure. Only when I buy something, say at the butcher's, I place my legs quite close together and parallel and don't move from the spot. That makes an upper-class impression, and I always get the best cut and the freshest calf's liver. (*He yawns.*) Have you noticed that I no longer yawn as unceremoniously as I used to, but with a pursed mouth, like you?

QUITT

The long and short of it: you are still here for me?

HANS

Because I am compelled to be as free as you are. You have everything, live only for yourself, don't have to make any comparisons any more. Your life is poetic, Mr. Quitt, and poetry, as we know, produces a sense of power that oppresses no one—but rather dances the dance of freedom for us, the oppressed. At one time I felt caught in the act even when someone watched me licking stamps. Now I don't bat an eyelash when someone calls me a lackey; carry the garbage can out onto the sidewalk in my tails absolutely unfazed; walk self-confidently arm in arm with the ugliest woman; do work, willy-nilly, which isn't mine to do—that is my freedom, which I have learned from you. In the past I used to be envious of what you could afford to do. I didn't feel treated like a man but like a mannequin—notice my new freedom, I'm already playing with words!—cursed you under my breath as a bloodsucker, did not see the human being in you, but only the corporation mogul. That's how unfree I was. Now, as soon as I imagine you, I see the self-assured curve that your watch chain describes over your belly and already I am moved.

QUITT

This sounds familiar. (HANS *laughs.*) So you're just making fun of me. I should have known that someone with your history would never change. But you're not the one who matters. It's the others that count.

HANS

Do you actually despise yourself, Mr. Quitt?— Now that you've screwed them all?

QUITT

Myself? No. But I might despise someone *like* me. (*Long pause.*) Why don't you react? Just now when you weren't answering me, what I said began to crawl back into me and wanted to make itself unsaid, and me too, by shriveling me deep inside. (*Pause.*) You're making fun of my language. I would much prefer to express myself inarticulately like the little people in the play recently, do you remember? Then you would finally pity me. This way I suffer my articulateness as part of my suffering. The only ones that you and your kind pity are those who can't speak about their suffering.

HANS

How do you want to be pitied? Even if you became speech-less with suffering your money would speak for you, and the money is a fact and you—you're nothing but a conscious-ness.

QUITT

(*Derisively*) Pity only occurred to me because the char-acters in the play moved me so—not that they were speech-less, but that despite their seemingly dehumanized demeanor they wanted really to be as kind to each other as we spectators who all live in more human surroundings are already with each other. They, too, wanted tenderness, a life together, et cetera—they just can't express it, and that is why they rape and murder each other. Those who live in in-human conditions represent the last humans on stage. I like that paradox. I like to see human beings on the stage, not monsters. Human beings, gnarled with suffering, unsche-matic, drenched with pain and joy. The animalistic attracts me, the defenseless, the abused and insulted. Simple people, do you understand? Real people whom I can feel and taste, living people. Do you know what I mean? People! Simply . . . people! Do you know what I mean? Not fakes but . . .

(*He thinks for quite a while.*) people. You understand: people. I hope you know what I mean.

HANS

I can't take your jokes so soon after waking up. But let's suppose you're being serious. There must be another possibility which makes your dichotomy—here fakes, there human beings—look ridiculous.

QUITT
Which?

HANS
I don't know.

QUITT
Why not?

HANS
That I don't know is the very thing that lends me hope. Besides, as one of those whom you have in mind: I can say it: every time when the curtain rises I become discouraged at the prospect that things will be human again up there any moment now. Let's further assume that you mean what you say: perhaps the people on stage moved you—not because they were people, but because everything was shown as it is. For example, if you recognize a portrait as true to life, you frequently develop a peculiar sympathy for the person in the portrait without necessarily having any feeling for the real person. Couldn't the same thing have happened to you when you saw the play? That you empathized with the inarticulate people represented there on the stage and think, therefore, that you have done with the real ones? And why do you want to see real characters on stage at all, who belong in the past and are alien to you?

QUITT
Because I like to think back to the days when I was poor too, and couldn't express myself, and primarily because the painted grimaces from my own class sit in the audience anyway. On stage I want to see the other class, as crude and as unadorned as possible. After all, I go to the theater to relax.

HANS
(*Laughs.*) So, you *are* being derisive.

QUITT
I meant that seriously. (*He laughs. Both of them laugh.*)

(WIFE *enters.*)

HANS
Here comes one of your real people.

WIFE
Are you laughing at me?

QUITT
Who else?

WIFE
And what were you saying about me?

HANS
Nothing. We were only laughing about you.

(WIFE *laughs too; she slaps* QUITT *on the shoulder, nudges him in the ribs.*)

QUITT
We're all merry for once, right?

HANS
Since business is so good, Mr. Quitt—why don't you cross my palm with silver?

QUITT
You're welcome.

(*He wants to put the coin into* HANS's *outstretched hand but* HANS *pulls back the hand and stretches out the other. Now* QUITT *wants to put the coin into that hand, but* HANS, *so as to adjust to* QUITT, *has already stretched out his first hand again. When he notices that* QUITT . . . *he stretches out his second hand again. But* QUITT *tries to put the coin into* HANS's *first hand again and in the meantime, etc. Until* QUITT *puts the coin away again, walks to the piano, and plays a boogie.* WIFE *takes* HANS *and dances with him . . . Then* QUITT *suddenly plays a slow, sad blues and sings along with it.*)

QUITT
Sometimes I wake up at night
and everything I want to do next day
suddenly seems silly,
how silly to button your shirt,
how silly to look in your eyes,
how silly the foam on the glass of beer,
how silly to be loved by you.

Sometimes I lie awake
and everything I imagine
makes everything that much more inconceivable—
inconceivable the pleasure of standing at a hot-dog stand,
inconceivable New Zealand,
inconceivable thinking of sooner or later,
inconceivable to be alive or dead

I want to hate you and hate plastic,
you want to hate me and hate the fog.
I want to love you and love hilly countrysides,
you would like to love me
and have a lovely city, a lovely color, a lovely animal.

Everyone stay away from me,
it is the time after my death
and what I just imagined, with a sigh, as my life
are only blisters on my body
which sigh when they burst

(*He stops singing.*) But things are going well for us right
now, aren't they? I saw a woman walking in the sun with a
full shopping bag and I knew at once: Nothing more can
happen to me now! I hear an old lady say: "Parsley on the
stalk? I've never eaten that." And then she says: "Well,
and I don't think I'll indulge in it now." Nothing can happen
to me any more! Nothing can happen to me any more! (*He
continues to sing.*)

No dream
could make anything seem stranger
than what I've already experienced
and there's no cure
for the peace and quiet

(*He speaks again.*) . . . with which every morning I let
the dingaling out from behind my fly to fidget in the peep
show to relieve the pressure which I could no longer imagine
during the sleepless night. (VON WULLNOW, KOERBER-KENT,
and LUTZ *appear silently.* WIFE *wants to leave.*) Stay here.
(*She leaves.* HANS *leaves too. Pause.*) So you still exist.
(*Pause.*) Why don't we make ourselves comfortable?
(*Pause.*) What can I offer you? Schnapps? Cognac?

KOERBER-KENT
No, thank you. It's still too early for that.

QUITT
Or juice, freshly squeezed.

KOERBER-KENT
That doesn't agree with my stomach. Hyperacidity.

QUITT
Then a few breadsticks. Or would you prefer some other snack?

LUTZ
Thank you, we really don't want anything. Seriously, don't go to any trouble.

QUITT
You've got a frog in your throat. Hans will make you a camomile tea. (LUTZ *shakes his head.*) Camomile which we picked ourselves at the Mediterranean. The blossoms are intact!

LUTZ
(*Clears his throat.*) I'm over it already. I don't need anything.

QUITT
And you, Monsignore? Perhaps you'd like a mint lozenge? One hundred percent pure peppermint.

KOERBER-KENT
I'm perfectly happy too.

QUITT
I'd put it on your tongue myself.

KOERBER-KENT
I usually enjoy sucking on mint lozenges, but not today.

QUITT
Why not today? It isn't Friday, is it?

KOERBER-KENT
I simply don't want to. That's all.

QUITT
You want to jilt me?

KOERBER-KENT
If that's how you take it.

QUITT
I'm offended.

(*He walks out.* KOERBER-KENT *wants to make a gesture to stop him but* VON WULLNOW *makes a sign not to.*)

VON WULLNOW
I know. I could cut off his head with one slash of the whip and let the decapitated chicken slap on the table before you. I was grinding my teeth so fiercely just now, some must have cracked. (*He shows his teeth.*) There! You traitor, you upstart, you Polack! (*Raving*) My hand even trembled briefly, which almost never happens to me. In the meantime, of course, it has become completely steady again. Look! (*He holds out his hand.*) But we have to be rational now, in the most economic sense of the word: at first as rational as necessary and then, when he no longer has any need for our reason, as irrational as possible. I'm already looking forward to my irrationality. (*He makes a pantomime of trampling, torturing, and throttling.*)

LUTZ

(*Interrupts him.*) Yes, that's it; we have to let ourselves go for a moment. Like you just now. Perhaps that'll teach us what to do next. Let's say or do whatever comes to mind. That will determine our method. After all, that's the way he does it. So let's dream. (*Pause. They concentrate. Pause.*) Nothing is happening. I only see myself cutting a steak against the grain or playing tennis in such short pants that my testicles are hanging out on one side. (*Pause. They concentrate.*) Do you know what I'm most afraid of about myself? (*They regard him expectantly.*) That one day I will get up in a restaurant so lost in thought that I forget to pay the check.

(*Pause.* KOERBER-KENT *scratches his behind and they regard him.*)

KOERBER-KENT

I just happened to think of our minority stockholder . . .

(*Pause.*)

LUTZ

Don't you ever dream?

KOERBER-KENT

Ah! Monstrous dreams!

LUTZ

Well! Let's hear.

KOERBER-KENT

(*Powerfully*) I . . . I'm walking in the woods alone . . .

(*Long, embarrassed silence. Pause.* VON WULLNOW *laughs.*)

LUTZ
You are laughing?

VON WULLNOW
I was remembering.

LUTZ
Was it that funny?

VON WULLNOW
Remembering it was. (*Pause.*) The grain bins in the loft, the trickling grain and the mouse shit inside, the swirl of grain that my memory delved into like a boy's naked foot, the grains between the toes, the vacated wasp nest, still so enlivened by memories, on the underside of the roof tile. (*Pause.*) I've got to stop. Remembering makes me a good person. Otherwise I would make up in a moment. Oh, Quitt. Oh, Quitt, why hast thou forsaken us?

LUTZ
Now I know what we are going to do. We have to talk about ourselves, about us as individuals—what we're really like. I for one sometimes feel like hopping up and down on the street and don't do it. Why not? And last summer passed by without my having enjoyed it once while I was sitting in my office with its tinted window. Every so often I do something crazy: I eat the rotten part of an apple, slam a car door before everyone's gotten out . . . or something like that . . . and if that doesn't help, there's always . . . (*To* KOERBER-KENT) our minority stockholder. (QUITT *returns.*) He'll show him where the moon is rising.

QUITT
I do miss you. And perhaps you miss me too.

VON WULLNOW

Quitt, today I had a bag of flour in my hand. Do you know how long it has been since I've held flour in my hands? I don't even know myself. The package was so soft and heavy. This weight in my hand and at the same time the gentleness of the pressure—I was transported into delicious unreality. Doesn't the same thing ever happen to you?

QUITT

I find the most vicious reality more bearable than the most delicious feeling of unreality.

LUTZ

(*Trying to distract*) How is your wife?

QUITT

My wife? My wife is fine.

LUTZ

She looked well just now. With her cheeks all rosy as though she'd just played tennis. That made me think of my wife, who has to rock the child all day long on the terrace. You know, we have a retarded child who screams as soon as we stop rocking: my wife stands days on end in the garden and pushes the swing, imagine that. But she's gotten to like doing it nowadays. She says that it calms her down too. And she feels it makes her superior to the other women in the neighborhood who can't think of anything to do but tell their cleaning women how to do chores. By the way, excuse me for talking about myself.

QUITT

I like women who do nothing but give orders.

VON WULLNOW

I know you like hearing stories, I have one.

QUITT
Is it long?

VON WULLNOW
Very brief. A child walks into a shop and says, "Six rolls, the *Daily News*, and three salt sticks!"

QUITT
Go on.

VON WULLNOW
That's the story.

(*Pause.*)

QUITT
It's beautiful.

VON WULLNOW
(*Suddenly embraces him vehemently.*) I knew you would like it. I knew it. I'm usually too shy to touch anyone, but this time I simply must. (*He pulls* QUITT's *cuffs out of his jacket, takes his hand.*) I've been looking at this dirty fingernail all the time—now I have to clean it for you. (*He does so, using his own fingernail, steps back.*) I don't know what's the matter with me. I'm blissed out with memories recently. Do you remember that time we dressed up as workers at the opera ball? With red bandanas, T-shirts, high-pegged pants, and muddy boots. The way we stepped on the ladies' toes? The way we scratched our crotches? Staring at everything, our mouths agape? Ordered Crimean champagne and drank out of the bottle? And at the end pushed our caps back and sang the "Internationale"?

QUITT
Crimean champagne is an illegal label. It should be called "Sparkling Wine from the Crimea." (*Pause.*) Yes, we

played the part very expertly, so that we could only play ourselves.

VON WULLNOW
And now you're in cahoots with them.

QUITT
How so?

VON WULLNOW
By thinking only of yourself. The huge share of the market which you control provides the enemies of the free-enterprise system, who are our enemies too, with the welcome opportunity—

LUTZ
(*Interrupts him. Quickly*) Not like that. (*To* QUITT) I've been thinking a lot about death lately. Everything I encounter looks like a sign to me. When I read in the papers "Next Wednesday, junk collection," then I sense at once: "That junk, that's me." Recently when I entered a tobacco shop somewhere out in the country I saw an obituary pinned up on the wall—and under the obituary lay a filthy, shriveled-up glove: that leather glove, that'll soon be me, my heart fluttered.

QUITT
And I recently saw an empty plastic bag in a hallway with the legend "Hams from Poland" on it. Should that have been a sign too? In any event, I suddenly felt incredibly safe when I read that.

LUTZ
Don't you ever think of death?

QUITT
I can't.

VON WULLNOW
(*Strikes his fist against his forehead.*) And I can't any more!
I'd like to open a newspaper now and read the word *asshole*
in it. This jungle. This slime. This swamp. These will-o'-the-
wisps. (LUTZ *has nudged him with his elbow and* VON WULL-
NOW *calms down.*) These will-o'-the-wisps above the swamp
when we used to walk home in fall after our dancing lessons!
Wanda on my arm, I could feel her goose bumps through
her blouse, and a pheasant screamed in its sleep as I kissed
her—an ugly word actually, kissing—only the cracks of our
lips touch each other, as unfeeling as peeled-off bark. (*Pause.*
VON WULLNOW *looks at* LUTZ, *who gives him the cue by
forming the word* nature *with his lips.*) Why nature? Of
course, I was about to talk about nature: it was nature that
made me aware—by teaching me how to perceive. Houses,
streets, and I were just a daydream at first, dreamer and
what he dreamed were in the same bubble where the
dreamer—hypnotized by the invariably same, never-changing
spot on the buckling house wall, grown together in his sleep
with the same street curve day in and day out—also con-
sidered himself part of his dream. Dark spots inside me as
the only thing undefined. Then the bubble burst and the
dark spots *inside* me unfolded like the forests *outside* me.
Only then did I begin to define myself as well. Not the
civilization of house and street, but *nature* made me aware of
myself—by making me aware of nature. So: only in the per-
ception of nature, not in the hallucinatory hodgepodge of
the objects of civilization, can we arrive at our own history.
But nowadays most people have become so civilized that
they simply dismiss rapport with nature as some kind of
withdrawal into childhood—although it is children whom
one keeps having to make artificially aware of nature—or,

even if they pretend to have rapport with nature, cannot endure this nature without the mirage of civilization: inside the forest they have no feeling for the forest; except from the perspective of the window of their terraced house which they designed and built themselves, and which they would immediately sell to someone—only then would the same forest be an experience of nature for them. You're going to ask me what I mean by all this.

QUITT
No.

VON WULLNOW
I mean to say that you, you with your ruthless overexpansion, are destroying our nature. You senselessly transform the old countryside where we could come to our senses into construction sites. Your blind department stores squat like live bombs in our old city centers. Every day a new branch goes up, differing from the others only by its tax identification number, which you even set up in neon light to blink from its roof as an advertisement of your sense of public responsibility!

QUITT
A good idea, isn't it?

VON WULLNOW
You're ruining our reputation by carrying on just the way the Joneses think a businessman behaves.

QUITT
Perhaps it's not our reputation I'm ruining but you.

VON WULLNOW
You know neither honor nor shame. The manure pit behind my country house is too good for you. I'd like to choke you

by stuffing blotting paper down your throat. I damn you!
Whosoever utters your name before me, there shall I reach
into his mouth and rip out his tongue, and with my very
own hands in fact. Wait, I'm going to step on your foot.
(*He does so, not that* QUITT *reacts.* VON WULLNOW *blows up
his cheeks and slaps them with his hands. He bites the back of
his hand. He hits his head with his fist, quickly touches up his
hair.*) You've disappointed me, Quitt. It's a pity about you.
I liked you best of all. We've got so much in common. I
still admire you. Whenever I have to reach a decision I think
of what you would do under the same circumstances. (*He
screams*) You rat, you Judas, for twenty pieces of silver—

QUITT
Thirty, to be exact.

VON WULLNOW
Twenty, I say.

QUITT
(*To* KOERBER-KENT) But thirty is right, isn't it?

KOERBER-KENT
Yes, it was thirty pieces of silver. According to the latest
findings, it's a question of—

VON WULLNOW
(*Screaming*) Pervert! Atavist! (LUTZ *places a hand on his
shoulder.*) I once dreamed that we grew old together. Every
day we drove in a carriage through town, playing bridge.
And now all that is supposed to remain a dream? Let's stop
fighting each other, Quitt. It could be so beautiful—just the
four of us—that is, five, counting Mrs. Tax—and since all
the others have thrown in the towel in the meantime, we
lone wolves have become so big there's no longer any need
for arrangements. Those who help us into our coats after

our conferences could conduct our affairs for us. Let's not underbid each other any more.

QUITT

I underbid *you*. (VON WULLNOW *roars.*) Does it help?

VON WULLNOW

A hobnailed boot in your privates! Don't you understand me! What am I at this moment? A radical! How I'd simply like to yawn at you. Do you have a slice of bread on you?

QUITT

Are you hungry?

VON WULLNOW

I'd like to have something to crumble between my fingers. My brain is scraping against my brain pan. Actually a pleasant sensation. So animalistic. (*To* LUTZ) I won't say anything more now. (*To* QUITT) I'd like to switch with you, you shark. Besides, it's time for your wife to pass through the room again, isn't it? Come on, say something, I'd like to have something to laugh about! Dear Hermann . . . (*Pause. He takes* QUITT's *arm.*) You know, I could be your father? Let's go fishing together, fathers always take their sons fishing. Up the stream before the thunderstorm hits. I'd like to be drunk now so that I could remember something. (*He lets go of* QUITT's *arm.*) Apropos streams. You ruin them with your plastic monsters, let the countryside choke on plastic still lives stamped "biodegradable" where no environment is even left or, at most, a multicolored mildew on the ground, a soot-colored dust on a sweetly crinkling leaf, a fish belly in the churning water. Do you know what children ask when they're actually shown a big ripe tomato? Is it made of plastic? they ask. And I personally saw a child that didn't want to sit down in a Rolls-Royce because the seat wasn't made of plastic. Let's stop all this overexpansion,

Hermann—or let's limit ourselves to products for environmental protection. There's still a pretty penny to be made in that field. Everything could be the way it used to be.

QUITT

But you stopped expanding a long time ago. Besides, as you say so rightly, the functional units are diminishing in size. So the number of units can continue to increase, right? I'm not the kind of man who wants to leave everything the way it is. I can't see anything without wanting to utilize it. I want to make everything I see into something else. And so do you! Except that you can't any more.

VON WULLNOW

(*Steps away from* QUITT.) You refuse to understand us.

QUITT

I understand you very well. You know what it means when one of us becomes human or even speaks about death. An emotion, after the first moment of fright, becomes a method for us.

VON WULLNOW

It's not that I call your behavior treason—but what should I call it? Faithlessness? Treachery? Unreliability? Falseness? Cuntiness? Disloyalty?

QUITT

Those are the expressions you apply to employees. Among us I would call it businesslike behavior.

VON WULLNOW

Now I really won't say anything more. I'll stick my finger down my throat in front of you. (*Does so and leaves, but returns at once.*) And I really was attached to you. (*He leaves and returns.*) You with your frog's body. (*He leaves and returns.*) My spit is too good for you. All I'll do is spit it from the back to the front of my mouth. (*Does so, leaves once more, returns once more, is beside himself, makes a horrible face, and leaves once and for all.*)

(LUTZ *wants to say something.*)

QUITT
I know what you want to say.

LUTZ
Then you say it.

QUITT
It's true. I didn't stick to our agreement.

LUTZ
But you didn't plan it that way.

QUITT
I simply forgot about it, did I?

LUTZ
Not exactly forgot perhaps, but you didn't take it seriously enough.

QUITT
Why should I have taken it seriously?

LUTZ
(*Laughs.*) Not bad. Very tricky indeed . . . (*Pause.*) Excuse me, I interrupted you. You were going to say something.

QUITT
No, that was it.

LUTZ

Once I begin to speak everything is completely thought out. I don't stutter. (*To* KOERBER-KENT) He multiplied his share of the market at our expense. I have nothing against his methods, but he should have discussed them with us. And besides, of course I do have something against his methods: he recruits the ex-convicts away from us in the labor market and promises them a sympathetic environment—and that means that he leaves them entirely to themselves in a certain area of production and pays all of them the same low wages. As he admitted just now, he manufactures smaller and smaller amounts of his products but without changing the size of the package, so that the buyers believe they're getting the same amount. This way his prices appear to remain the same while we have to raise ours. He lets doctors buy shares in his drug firms and then they prescribe his medicines. (*To* QUITT) You duplicate our most expensive products with cheap materials. Your guarantees are only valid for Three-Star refrigerators. You print the national eagle on your retail price tags, so that it looks as though they are government-approved. Your price tags are huge—so that people believe your things are cheaper even when they are at least as expensive as anywhere else. The price structure has cracked, Quitt. We are standing at the deathbed—at the deathbed of the old concept of price—and have gotten sore feet ourselves. We shiver in the shadow of your competition. As far as I'm concerned, I'm still far too calm. Perhaps that is the calm before the next breach of the agreement, which will be my downfall. I can already see the hailstorm in the distance, and panic flattens my ears against my head. I'm afraid, Quitt, afraid of the great storm when I won't be wearing the thick coat of capital. And yet I tried to save the structure by firing thousands. Quitt, you ruined our prices. You pushed them down to prewar levels! Everything has a slight crack. Every day there's one product less on the market. It's all over with the beautiful diversity of the market. Even the high consecration is for nothing. It's the end of all our proud figures. I'm at a loss. I am at a most poodle-befuddled loss and in utter despair. (*To* KOERBER-KENT) I was my parents' only child. Even my birth was a practical decision: it meant my mother's death. At age four I kneaded imitation coins out of mud. At age seven I picked flowers for invalids in the neighborhood and sold them. In school they called me "Moneybags." A sensible boy, my father said. He still has respect for material values, said my relatives. Before my first communion, the priest said that if you really wanted something afterward and really believed it, the wish would come true. Still feeling the pressure of the host against my gums, I walked all the way home with my head lowered: because every cell of my body believed I would find the coin I had wished for. (*To no one in particular*) Since that time I've had my doubts about religion. (*To* KOERBER-KENT) But I remained reasonable and became more and more reasonable. He's all business, people said of me. But now it's all over. All over. I don't want to believe anything any more. What's there left to believe in if that s.o.b. destroys our prices and our rational system? What kind of age is that? What's still valid? I too want to be unbusinesslike at last! (*Pause.*) I dreamed that I was running and kept on running so that a huge banknote wouldn't fall off my chest. Just the way I keep on talking now. I'd like to put my head into a bowl of water and drown myself. (*Exit.*)

(KOERBER-KENT *wants to follow him but returns again.* QUITT *paces up and down.*)

KOERBER-KENT
(*With lowered head*) I don't envy you, Quitt. I could also tell you about myself, like the others, but that's not my way. I never talk about myself. I'm proud that I eliminated myself from my own calculations long ago. I'm not interested in

poking around the lint in my navel. I'm glad that I can be replaced. (*Pause.*) I pity you, Quitt. And I'm afraid for you. I recently saw a drawing a painter made of his dying wife: the pupils had lost almost all their color in the fever, and the iris, too, had become very pale. Nothing but a dark circle separated it from the white of the eye around it, and the centrifugal force of dying had even thickened this circle. It was as if the eyes sighed toward the observer. The artist's pencil had hatched an endless sea of sighs from a mortal seeing hole, as I called it. And the following morning the woman is supposed to have really died. (*A popping sound backstage.*) What was that?

QUITT

Hans is at work. He isn't very good at uncorking bottles. There's almost always a pop when he opens the cooking wine.

(*Pause.*)

KOERBER-KENT

Aren't you afraid to die? (*He raises his head and wants to transfix* QUITT—*but* QUITT *happens to be standing behind him.*)

QUITT
Over here.

KOERBER-KENT

Don't you ever quickly push everything away from you just because you are deathly afraid? (QUITT *steps away from him and comes to a halt with his back to him.* KOERBER-KENT *lowers his head again and closes his eyes.*) Someone once told me how he dreamed he was dying. He was sitting on a sled and said: I am dying. Then he was dead, and at some point they closed the coffin lid over him. And only then did he become deathly afraid: he didn't want to be buried. He woke up, his heart was fibrillating. Besides, he was very ill, the dream wanted to kill him. Cause of death: a dream, you could say. (*Very loudly*) You see, dying in your sleep isn't at all peaceful, but perhaps the worst death of all.

(QUITT *has kept pacing around in the meantime, absentmindedly, and now stands in front of* KOERBER-KENT.)

QUITT
(*Very softly*) Really?

KOERBER-KENT
(*Is startled. Looks up at* QUITT *now.*) I know from other stories (*One can hear a key turning in a lock backstage and a door handle being pressed down.*) that a dying person keeps looking away whenever his eye catches a specific object, as though he could postpone death in this way . . . (*He listens.*) Someone pushed down a door handle just now, no? Why don't I hear a door opening? (*Pause.*) Once during a meal I personally sat opposite a man who suddenly started putting the table in order: put the knife and fork parallel to each other, wiped the edge of the glass with his napkin, shoved the napkin into its silver ring. Then he keeled over dead.

QUITT
(*Distracted*) Who kneeled on the bread?

KOERBER-KENT
He keeled over dead, I said. (*Frightened*) You're afraid too.

QUITT
(*Scratching his pants absentmindedly*) Damnit, the cleaner didn't get that spot out either. Yes? I'm listening.

KOERBER-KENT

He was still smiling beforehand—(*Two or three distinctly audible steps backstage.*) but in his deathly fear he bared his *lower* teeth instead of his upper teeth, as you would expect. Nothing wrong with a dead dwarf, that's still a vegetative process, almost. But a *fully grown* corpse, just imagine that! It's monstrous. (*He listens.*) Why doesn't he walk on? Wasn't someone just walking back there?

QUITT

My baby fat starts growing back when I listen to you. You and your deathly fear—at the moment everything seems thinkable to me and also beside the point.

KOERBER-KENT
What? What?

QUITT
It was just the floor creaking, I'm sure of it.

(PAULA *appears in a dress and with a veil in front of her face. At the sight of her,* QUITT *unzips his fly halfway down and up again. A garbage can cover bangs loudly on a hard floor backstage.*)

KOERBER-KENT

As I said, I've got an eye for those who are marked. (*He points to* QUITT.) It's that thin line on the upper lip . . . (*He notices* PAULA.) It's you! How good that you are here. Perhaps you could . . . him . . . (*He tries to find the word.*) What's the word?

QUITT
Congratulate him?

KOERBER-KENT
No.

QUITT
Work on him?

KOERBER-KENT
Something like that . . . no.

QUITT
Take him over your knees?

KOERBER-KENT
(*Panic-stricken*) Oh, God, how did this happen? I can't find
the right word any more. What are they doing to me? Come
down, eclipse of the sun! Hellfire, burst forth from the earth!

(QUITT *walks up to* PAULA *and whispers in her ear.*)

PAULA
(*Loudly*) "Deathly afraid?" (*To* KOERBER-KENT) You are
trying to make him deathly afraid? Do you think he'll admit
us back into the market?

KOERBER-KENT
(*Screams*) I know what I'm talking about. I've seen thousands die in the war. (QUITT *sighs.* KOERBER-KENT *resumes
normal tone of voice at once.*) Am I keeping you from something?

QUITT
Not at all.

KOERBER-KENT
(*Screams*) I can read signs. I know why you hunch up your
shoulders when you walk around. But soon you will shoulder
the necessary weight of death, no matter what, Hermann
Quitt. Even if you dangle your arms back and forth like that
and scurry every which way. Even if you sit up straight as a

candle in your deathly fear! (*He begins walking out back-ward.* HANS *appears, wearing his chef's hat.*) You won't even be able to imagine the moment. There will be nothing but abrupt, animalistic, anxiety-ridden anticipation. You will be so afraid you won't even dare to swallow, and the spit will turn sour in your mouth. Your death will be gruesome beyond all imaginings, complete with moaning and bellowing. I know what I'm talking about. With moaning and bellowing. (*He walks backward into* HANS *and emits a scream. Exit.*)

(HANS *also exits.* QUITT *and* PAULA *look at one another for a long time.*)

QUITT
If you keep looking at me, I will lose the rest of my feelings.

PAULA
I won.

QUITT
Why?

PAULA
Because you were the first to talk.

QUITT
Now it's your turn.

PAULA
I love you, still. (*She laughs.*)

QUITT
Why are you laughing?

PAULA
Because I succeeded in saying that.

QUITT

I can't buy myself anything with that.

PAULA

You are so artificial. You're sacrificing the truth now for a slick cliché.

QUITT

Moreover, I didn't give you any excuse for it. (*Pause.*) I keep having to get used to you all over again. (*He looks her over from head to foot.*)

PAULA

I'm not one of those.

QUITT

Who, after all, is one of those? (*Pause.*) I'm tired. When I take a step I feel as if my real body has stayed behind. I don't need you. When I saw you I was happy, but I also was a bit turned off. I took that as a sign that all my desire for you is gone.

(*She laughs. He regards her considerately until she has finished.*)

PAULA

What you say is supposed to humiliate me. But the voice that I hear flatters me.

QUITT

You've changed. You're out of breath. Before, when you used to show your feelings you used to be much more self-assured. Why can't it be that way now? Stop playing the humble woman. I only want to touch you when you talk matter-of-factly. (*Spitefully*) Incidentally, why are you by yourself and not with the team? Do you call that creative?

My head hurts. Besides, I like you better when you wear pants.

PAULA
Your head is also hurting me, yes, your whole life . . . (QUITT *pats her arm.*) You pat me the way a conductor raps his baton . . . (*She caresses him.*)

QUITT
Your caresses tickle me.

PAULA
Yes, because you don't want to enjoy them. (QUITT's WIFE *enters. She is wearing the same dress as* PAULA. *She notices, stops, and leaves again.*) Now caress me too. (QUITT *caresses her and steps away from her.*) That was one too few. (QUITT *returns and caresses her once more.*) Oh yes. (*Pause.*) Tell me about yourself.

QUITT
(*Animatedly*) I was thirsty a few days ago. (*Pause.*) It just occurred to me.

PAULA
Look at me, please.

QUITT
I don't like to look at you.

PAULA
Well, what am I like?

QUITT
Unchanged.

PAULA

Before I got to know you better I thought you were unfeeling and tough. I once heard you say of me—the brunette there—as about a whore.

QUITT

You always tell yourself stories like that afterward.

PAULA

What would you say I would say now? Mr. Quitt?

QUITT

Don't call me that. (*She puts her hand on his shoulder. Suddenly she begins to choke him. He lets her do so for some time, then shakes her off.* QUITT'S WIFE *has returned in a different dress. She watches, giggling inaudibly, sucking her thumb.* QUITT *seats himself in the deck chair and lowers his head.* PAULA *squats down and wants to take his head in her hands. He gives her a kick. She falls down and gets up, warbling. He kicks her again. She gets up, warbling. He wants to kick her again, but she eludes him, warbling.*) Your slimy tongue. Your absurd hips.

PAULA

(*Lifts her dress.*) Look at the way my thigh is twitching. Can you see it? Why don't you come closer? (QUITT *grunts.*) Come on.

(QUITT *puts his hand on her thigh.* PAULA *presses her head close to him. Pause.*)

QUITT

All right, get lost now. (*He steps back. Pause.*) The saliva in your mouth will run over in a moment. And the way your eyeballs jerk back and forth! (*He turns away. Pause.*)

PAULA

I'm going already. It's no use. I'll sell.

QUITT

(*Regards her.*) And I'll determine the fine print.

PAULA

Only promise me that you won't clean up the moment after I've left.

QUITT

Buying yourself a hat can be very comforting.

PAULA

Now I know why I like you. It's so easy to think of something else when you're talking.

QUITT

Tomorrow at this time it will already be lighter, or darker. Perhaps that will comfort you too.

PAULA

(*Suddenly embraces* QUITT's WIFE, *releases her, and tosses* QUITT *a friendly as well as a serious kiss as she walks out.*) "No hard feelings . . ."

(QUITT *throws a stool after her.* PAULA *exits.*

QUITT's WIFE *comes closer. They stand opposite each other, not saying anything. The stage light changes after some time. First sunshine, then cloud shadows moving across the two of them. Crickets chirp. Far off in the distance a dog barks. The sound of the ocean. A child screams something into the wind. Distant church bells. Woolly tree blossoms blow across the stage. Both of them as silhouettes in the dusk against the backdrop of city lights, which are just coming on. The noise of an airplane engine, very close, slowly receding—while previous stage lighting comes back on. Quiet.*)

WIFE
(*Softly*) You look so unapproachable.

QUITT
Remembering does that. I'm just remembering. Let me be. I've got to remember to the end. (*He sits down on the deck chair. She steps closer. He touches her lightly with his foot.*)

WIFE
Yes?

QUITT
Nothing, nothing. (*He leans back and closes his eyes.*)

WIFE
(*Sighs.*) Oh.

QUITT
(*To himself*) So that it crashes and splinters . . .

WIFE
What will you do?

QUITT
(*To himself*) Stop. Destroy. (*He looks back at her.*) Strange: when I look at you, my thoughts skip a beat.

WIFE
I'd like to speak about myself for once too.

QUITT
Not again!

WIFE
Why, are you listening to me?

QUITT
You could have been talking about yourself while you asked that. Did you wash your hair?

WIFE
Yes, but not for you. I am not well.

QUITT
Then scream for help.

WIFE
When I scream for help, you reply by telling me a story how you once needed help. (*Pause. She laughs a few times in quick succession as though about something funny.* QUITT *doesn't react.*) Help!

QUITT
You have to shout at least twice.

WIFE
I can't any more.

QUITT
(*Gets up.*) Then do away with yourself. (*He turns away.*)

WIFE
(*Mechanically wipes the dandruff off his shoulders.*) You're up to something. I can't look at you for too long, otherwise I'll find out what.

QUITT
What do you want? I have a pink face, my body is warm, pulse eighty.

(*Pause.*)

WIFE
My eyes are burning. I'm so sad I forgot to blink.

QUITT
What's there to eat today?

WIFE
Filet of veal with truffles.

QUITT
I see. Well, well. Interesting. *What* is there to eat today?

WIFE
But you just asked that. Why are you so distracted?

QUITT
(*To himself*) Because every possibility has been tried except the very last one, and that one shouldn't turn into just another idle mental exercise! Of course, filet of veal with truffles, you said so—I hear it only now. Why am I so distracted? I have to tell you something, my dear.

(*A pause. She looks at him.*)

WIFE
No, please don't say it. (*She shies back.*)

QUITT
I have to tell someone.

WIFE
(*Shies back and holds her ears shut.*) I don't want to hear it.

QUITT
(*Follows her.*) You'll know it in a moment.

WIFE

Don't say it, please don't. (*She runs away and he follows her. Quiet. Pause. She returns, slowly, walking backward, and goes off again, not that one sees her face.*)

(KILB *storms in.* HANS *appears behind him, wearing the chef's hat.* KILB *is holding a knife and runs back and forth.*)

KILB

You have to die now. It's no use. I'm alone. No one pays me. Not even they. It's our last way out. Don't contradict me. (*He notices that there's no one present, and puts the knife back in his pocket.*) He isn't even here! And I rehearsed it so well! Into the room and right at him! One, two. A picture without words, only dashes for the caption underneath.

HANS

You have to try again.

KILB

I have to concentrate once more for that. If I'm as unconcentrated as I am now, everything could just as easily be something else, I think, even I myself. And that is a hideous feeling. Leave me alone.

HANS

But look at me first: because it's really me now. People used to say about me: That fellow, it's eating him up inside, but one day he'll blow his stack and the walls will come tumbling down. That moment has come. So I will leave the room and cook the truffled filet with special tenderness, thinking how it will be left over for me. I leave Mr. Quitt to his fate, he believes in things like that. First of all, I'm going to stick to myself and I am curious what that will bring. My big toe is already itching, a good sign; I'm becoming human.

KILB
How?

HANS
Because an itching big toe means that you should remember
something, and someone who remembers becomes a human
being. So all I need to do is remember.

There was a time something inside me wanted to scream
At the mere thought that I might dream.
Now I want to learn to dream without end
So that the floor of facts I might transcend.
My eyes I want to learn to close
So as to know more of the little I knows.
In my youth a palm reader told me a fable
That I would be able
To change the world's plan.
I hereby announce that at least *my* world is changing.
(*He quickly punches the balloon punching-bag fashion. The
balloon bursts.* HANS *exits.*

    KILB *concentrates, puts the stool on its legs, gently closes
the cover of the piano, puts in order what needs putting into
order.*

    QUITT *returns.*)

KILB
Not yet!

QUITT
You again.

KILB
But we haven't seen each other in ages.

QUITT

Not ages enough. Recently I thought of a mistake I once made. I couldn't remember what kind of mistake it had been—but I was sure at once that it was not an important mistake. Later on I remembered more distinctly: it had been an important mistake after all. It occurred to me only when I was dealing with you.

KILB

Please stay like that.

(*Pause.*)

QUITT

Kilb, I'm happy that you came. And please note that I said "I'm happy" and not "it makes me happy."

KILB

Please don't become too friendly now. (*Pause.* QUITT *regards him for a long time.*) Why are you looking at me?

QUITT

I'm only too tired to look elsewhere. Why don't *you* at least sit down, so that I won't become even more tired. (*He points to the deck chair.*)

KILB

No, that's too deep for me, I'll never be able to get out of it. (QUITT *sits down in it.*) Particularly if you keep your hands in your pockets the way you do. *I* always keep my hands out of my pockets in moments of danger.

QUITT

Kilb, nothing is possible any longer. I feel like I'm the sole survivor, and I find it unappetizing that there's nothing left except me. If only there were an appetizing explanation for this state of affairs—but my awareness is the awareness of a pile of garbage in an infinite empty space. Imagine: the telephone no longer rings, the postman doesn't come any more, all street noises have ceased, only the wind is rustling one dream further away—the world has already died. I'm the only one who hasn't heard of the catastrophe. I'm actually only a phantom of myself. What I see are afterimages, what I think are afterthoughts. A hair bends over on my head and I'm frightened to death. The next moment will be the last and un-time will begin. Just a moment ago there was still a bubble where I was, but not any more. I know that my time is over. You were right, Paula.

KILB
Absolutely right. You're an anachronism, Mr. Quitt. Like the goose step of your soul right now.

QUITT
Be quiet. No one but I can say that. (*He bounces a little ball and looks at* KILB.) Now that it's just the two of us, instead of becoming different you only become afraid that you might become different. (*Pause.*) There is nothing unthought of any more. Even the Freudian slip from the unconscious has already become a management method. Even dreams are dreamed from the beginning so as to be interpretable. For example, I no longer dream anything that isn't articulated, and the pictures of the dream follow each other logically like the sequence of days in a diary. I wake up in the morning and am paralyzed with all the speeches I've heard in the dream. There's no longer the "and suddenly" of the old dreams. (*The ball escapes and rolls away.*) Oh, too bad . . . (*He gets up.* KILB *has approached.*) The chair really is too deep, you're right. When I think of myself, using precise concepts, I have one attack of nausea after the other. This businessman with a handkerchief in his breast pocket and his English worsted suit full of *Weltschmerz* on board his private

plane the soot from whose jets drifts down on the workers' apartment projects, with organ music of the Old Masters oozing from the built-in loudspeakers—stop it, get rid of it, bomb it, it's logical. But: every logical conclusion is immediately contradicted within me by this totally indecisive yet totally self-assured *feeling.*

KILB
It's logical. You want to go on living.

QUITT
The little man wants to put on airs.

KILB
Why not. What else has the little man left to put on?

QUITT
You're right. Why not? A good cue. I'm still stuck too deep in my role. Spitefully I walk past the spastics in the V.A. hospitals and look away when someone rummages in garbage cans for food. Why do I do it, actually? There's scarcely anyone who looks as if he could still fall out of his role. I once walked on the street and suddenly noticed that I didn't have anything to do with my face any more . . .

KILB
The old story with the masks.

QUITT
Yes, but now someone who experienced it is telling about it. Outside, the muscles clung to the dead skin, then one dead layer on top of the other, only inside, in the deepest center, where I should have been, there was still a little twitching and something wet. A car would have to crash into me at once!— Only then would I stop making a face. And not merely show my true face when I can't avoid the onrushing

I dance on the inside with self-awareness. Yes, inside I'm dancing! I once sat in the sun in actual shock, the sun was shining on me, not that I felt it, and I really felt like the outline of suffocating nothingness in the airy space around me. But even that was still me, me, me. I was in despair, could think neither back nor forward—had no sense of history left. Each recollection came in dribs and drabs, unharmoniously, like the recollection of a sex act. This aching lack of feeling, that was myself, and I was not only I but also a quality of the world. Of course, I asked about the terms. Why? Why this condition? These conditions—why no history but only these conditions? But all the conditional requirements were fulfilled. No "whys" helped any more. Only the unconditional requirements remained. "I'm bored," a child once said. "Then play at something. Paint something. Read something. Do something," it was told. "But I can't, I'm bored," it said. (*He keeps taking objects from his pockets, looks at them, and puts them back again.*) The goose step of my soul, you said? I want to speak about (*Laughs.*) myself without using categories. I don't want to mean anything any more, please, not be a character in the story any more. I want to freeze at night in May. Look, these are photos of me: I look happy in all of them and yet I never was. Do you know the feeling when one has put a pair of pants on backward? One time I was happy: when I visited someone in a tenement and during a long pause in the conversation I could hear the toilet flushing in the apartment next door. I became musical with happiness! Oh, my envy of your sleepy afternoons in those tenements with their mysteriously gurgling toilet bowls! Those are the places I long for: the projects at the edge of the city where the telephone booths are lit up at night. To go into airport hotels and simply check oneself in for safekeeping. Why are there no depersonification institutes? How beautiful it used to be when you opened a new can of shoe polish! And I could still imagine buying a ham sandwich, looking at cemeteries, having something in common with someone. Sometimes one thing simply led exhilaratingly to the other—that's what it meant to feel alive! Now I'm heavy and sore and bulky with myself. (*He punches himself under his chin while talking, kicks his calf.*) One wrong breath and I disintegrate. Do you know that I hear voices? But not the kind of voices that madmen hear: no religious phrases, or poetry regurgitated from schooldays, or one-shot philosophies, none of the traditional formulas— but movie titles, pop tunes, advertising slogans. "Raindrops are falling on my head," it frequently resounds in a whisper in the echo chamber of my head, and in the middle of an embrace a voice interrupts me with "Guess who's coming to dinner?" or "I'd walk a mile for a Camel." And I am positive that in the future even madmen will hear only voices like that—no longer "Know thyself" or "Thou shalt honor thy father and mother . . ." the superego voices of our culture. While one set of monsters is being exorcised, the next ones are already burping outside the window. (*He interrupts himself.*) How odd: while I go on talking logically like this, I simultaneously see, for example, a wintry lake at dusk which is just beginning to freeze over, or a small tree with a bottle stuck on its top, and an unshaven Chinese who peers around a doorway—now he's gone again—and, moreover, during the whole time I keep humming a certain moronic melody inside myself. (*He hums.* KILB *wants to say something.*) No, *I* am speaking now. I am blowing my horn! The goose step of my soul. You should try it too. At least try . . . Stand still, why don't you! Do I spit when I talk? Yes, I can feel the spit bubbles on my teeth. But my time to speak isn't over yet. At one time I used to think, Let's hope the next world war doesn't start before my new suit is ready. By talking I want to have the transmission of consciousness, now, before you are finished with me. For too long my lips have held themselves joylessly shut. (*He suddenly embraces* KILB *and holds on to him.*) Why am I talking so fluently? Whereas I actually feel the need to stutter. (*He bends over*

and therefore presses KILB *more tightly.* KILB *is writhing.*)
I w . . . want to s . . . stutter . . . And why do I see
everything so distinctly? I don't want to see the grain in the
wood floor so distinctly. I'd like to be nearsighted. I'd like
to tremble. Why am I not trembling? Why am I not
stuttering? (*He bends over vehemently and* KILB *writhes.*) I
once wanted to sleep. But the room was so big. Wherever I
lay down I created spots of sleeplessness. The room was too
big for me alone. Where is the place to sleep here? Smaller!
Smaller! (*He bends over so much that* KILB *groans. He bends
even more and the groaning ceases.* KILB *falls on the floor
and doesn't move.* QUITT *crosses his arms. Pause.*) I can smell
the cologne he smelled of. (*Pause.*) How happy I became
once when I put on a shirt one of whose buttons had just
been sewn on. My shirt is torn. How beautiful! Then I wore
it long enough for it to become threadbare.

(*Pause.
A tremendous burping pervades the entire room.
Long pause.
The burping.
*QUITT *runs his head against the rock. After some time he
gets up and runs against the rock again. He gets up once
more and runs against the rock. Then he just lies there. The
stage light has been extinguished. Only the trough with the
risen dough, the melting block of ice, the shriveled balloon,
and the rock are lighted. A fruit crate trundles down, as
though down several steps, and comes to rest in front of the
rock. A long gray carpet rolls out from behind the rock:
snakes writhe on the rolled-out carpet and in the fruit crate.*)

**Translated by MICHAEL ROLOFF
in collaboration with Karl Weber**